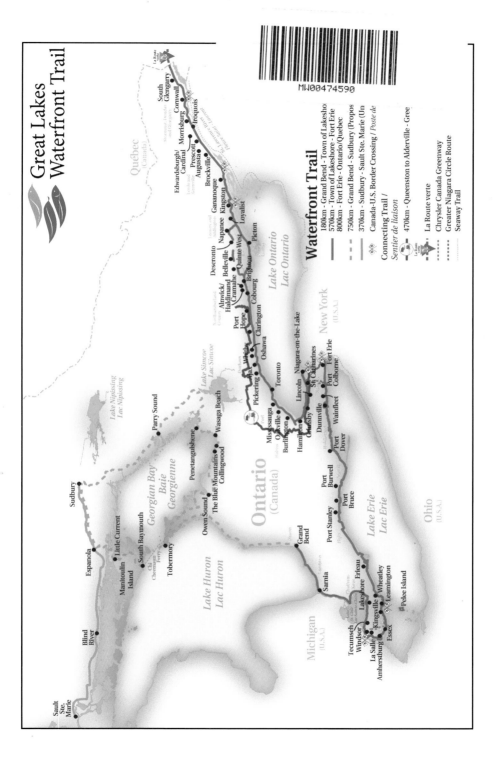

Great Lakes Waterfront Trail

MW00474590

Waterfront Trail

— 180km - Grand Bend - Town of Lakesho
— 570km - Town of Lakeshore - Fort Erie
— 800km - Fort Erie - Ontario/Quebec
- - - 750km - Grand Bend - Sudbury (Propos
- - - 370km - Sudbury - Sault Ste. Marie (Un

✳ Canada-U.S. Border Crossing / Poste de

Connecting Trail /
Sentier de liaison

✳ La Route verte

··········· 470km - Queenston to Alderville - Gree

······ La Route verte
- - - Chrysler Canada Greenway
········· Greater Niagara Circle Route
·········· Seaway Trail

Before you head off on your next adventure, head to us for handy travel resources.

Safe cycling tips:

Be visible. Use lights at night and in low light situations.

Be predictable. Signal your intentions and obey traffic signals and signs.

Be aware. Do not use headphones or mobile devices while driving or cycling.

bikesafety.caa.ca/cyclists

Get the FREE CAA Ontario Bike Assist App.

- CAA Members get one-touch access to Roadside Assistance for their bicycles*

- Browse cycling routes including the Waterfront Trail

- Share routes and view tutorials for common bike issues

Download the **CAA Ontario Bike Assist App**.

caasco.com/greatbikeassist

🚲 **5 h**
98.4 km

Looking for a great road trip?

CAA's **Drive/Ride Vacations** combine road trips, sightseeing and cycling trails into one amazing getaway.

Discover the best routes plus everything worth seeing along the way!

caasco.com/greatroadtrip

Great Lakes Waterfront Trail Mapbook-Ontario's Southwest Edition

Table of Contents

Great Lakes
Waterfront
Trail

Contact us:
Waterfront Regeneration Trust
4195 Dundas Street West, Ste 227
Toronto, Ontario M8X 1Y4
Tel. 416-943-8080
E-Mail: info@wrtrust.com

www.waterfronttrail.org

Published by:
LUCIDMAP
222 Islington Av., Ste 227
Toronto, ON M8V 3W7
Tel: 416-244-7881
E-Mail: info@lucidmap.ca
www.lucidmap.ca

Important note for trail users

There are inherent risks in hiking and cycling. Trail users use the information in this map book entirely at their own risk. The author and publisher disclaim any liability for any injuries or other damage incurred by anyone using the trails or information described in this publication.

These maps have been developed to assist Trail users in planning both their recreational and commuting trips along the Great Lakes Waterfront Trail. They show signed routes of the Trail, as well as possible routes and connections in areas where routes have not yet been designated as part of the Great Lakes Waterfront Trail.

The Great Lakes Waterfront Trail follows a variety of paths, streets and roads owned, managed or maintained by municipalities, conservation authorities, and the Province of Ontario. Some sections of the route may not be ideal for cycling or hiking. They may be unsuitable for some Trail users because of close proximity to vehicular traffic. Whenever possible, indicators have been placed on the maps to warn of caution areas. Be prepared to make your own evaluation of the traffic and road conditions, and plan routes appropriate to your riding and hiking skills and your comfort level. This map is not intended as a guide for children.

These maps have been digitally created based on various authoritative sources. Every reasonable care has been taken to ensure that the information is correct at the time of publication. No responsibility can be accepted for any mishap or damages arising from any inaccuracies, omissions or new developments within the mapped areas.

Reproducing or recording of maps or other material from this publication is strictly prohibited. The authors appreciate receiving feedback regarding inaccuracies, developments or comments.

Sixth Edition, 2016
ISBN10: 1-927391-94-5 /
ISBN13: 978-1927391945

All maps ©2016 LUC[D]MAP.
Other content ©2016 Waterfront Regeneration Trust.

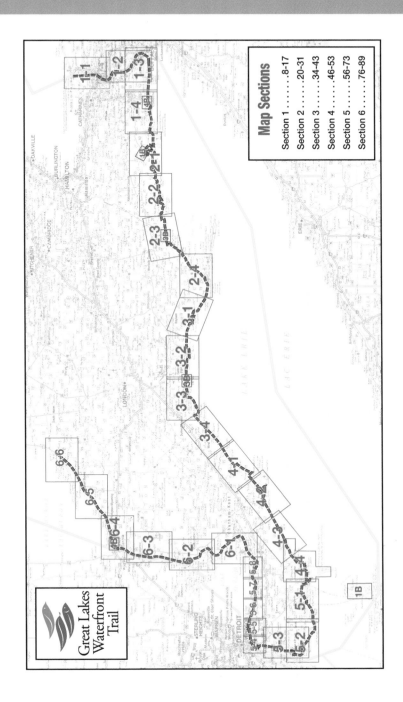

Map Sections

Section 1 8-17
Section 2 20-31
Section 3 34-43
Section 4 46-53
Section 5 56-73
Section 6 76-89

Great Lakes Waterfront Trail

Great Lakes Waterfront Trail

Canada's Great Lakes Waterfront Trail just keeps getting better.

www.waterfronttrail.org

Two decades ago, the Great Lakes Waterfront Trail was launched to celebrate and reconnect people to Canada's Great Lakes, the largest group of fresh-water lakes on earth. Then, it ran 270 kilometres from Hamilton to Trenton along Lake Ontario. Today, the fully-signed route welcomes walkers, runners, and cyclists to enjoy the Great Lakes from Grand Bend on Lake Huron to the Ontario/Quebec border on the St. Lawrence River. It is the signature project of the Waterfront Regeneration Trust, a charity working in partnership with over 100 community partners.

After 20 years of collaboration and connection the Great Lakes Waterfront Trail links 3 Great Lakes (Huron, Erie and Ontario), 4 bi-national rivers (St Clair, Detroit, Niagara and St. Lawrence), 3 UNESCO Biospheres, 20 Provincial Parks, 500+ parks, beaches, conservation areas and heritage attractions— among the finest Ontario has to offer. And the work is on-going with munici-palities undertaking projects every year to complete, connect and enhance the Great Lakes Waterfront Trail.

Ontario's Southwest Edition of the Great Lakes Waterfront Trail Mapbook

The 36 maps in this edition cover approximately 800 km of the Trail from Niagara to Lambton. Highlights include:

- 17% multi-use trails. Longest stretches of off-road trails are located in Sarnia/Point Edward and St. Clair Township along the St. Clair River Trail, Windsor's Ganatchio Trail, the Friendship Trail from Port Colborne to Fort Erie and the Niagara River Recreation Trail from Fort Erie to Niagara-on-the-Lake.
- 83% scenic rural roads and secondary highways; with some stretches of gravel roads.
- Pelee Island has 28 kilometres of very quiet roads to cycle—wonderful for families.
- Ferry service to:
    - Pelee Island from Leamington and Kingsville
    - Michigan, USA at Walpole and Sombra in St Clair Township
- Toronto to Windsor via the Great Lakes Waterfront Trail is 738 km.

The expansion of the Great Lakes Waterfront Trail into Ontario's Southwest was made possible through support from Ontario Government through the Great Lakes Community Guardian Fund, Tourism Development Fund, Ontario's Southwest Tourism, CAA, and donations from our Waterfront Trail Champions.

Visit www.waterfronttrail.org for:

On-line mapping resources, trip ideas, information about the work of the Waterfront Trail partnership

Ready. Set. Explore.

Plan your Ontario's Southwest Waterfront Trail travels in a few quick clicks

With scenic Lake Erie and Lake Huron shorelines, beautiful beaches, some of the continent's best birding, a rapidly evolving wine, craft beer and culinary scene and the friendliest communities on the planet, the most difficult part of your journey along the Great Lakes Waterfront Trail may be narrowing down your must-see list. Luckily, we can help with that.

OntariosSouthwest.com is your one-stop source for the travel information you need for all points of your journey along the trail between Dunnville and Grand Bend, including:

- Detailed descriptions of the region's best beaches, complete with recommendations for nearby excursions, lodging and restaurant options
- An interactive map of Canada's South Coast Birding Trail, highlighting the prime sites for experiencing the region's world-class birding
- Sample itineraries for experiencing the region's wineries, craft breweries, and outstanding farm-to-table fare
- Hundreds of listings for restaurants, hotels, bed and breakfasts, camp grounds and area attractions to incorporate into your Waterfront Trail travels
- Event listings so you can time your trip and experience the region's best festivals, fairs and fun
- Printable coupons and offers for great savings at local hotels, restaurants and attractions

Start planning your trip today at OntariosSouthwest.com

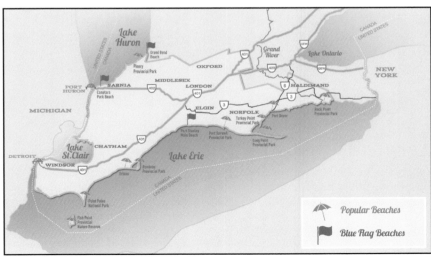

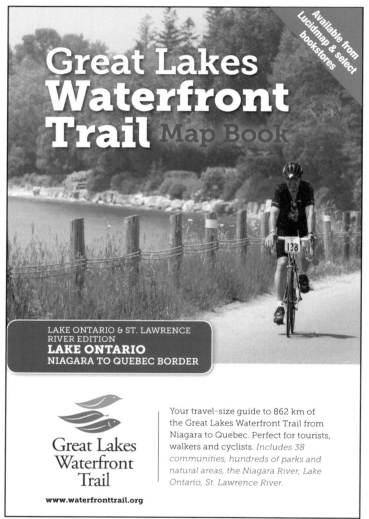

Available from Lucidmap & select bookstores

Great Lakes Waterfront Trail Map Book

LAKE ONTARIO & ST. LAWRENCE RIVER EDITION
LAKE ONTARIO
NIAGARA TO QUEBEC BORDER

Great Lakes
Waterfront
Trail

Your travel-size guide to 862 km of the Great Lakes Waterfront Trail from Niagara to Quebec. Perfect for tourists, walkers and cyclists. *Includes 38 communities, hundreds of parks and natural areas, the Niagara River, Lake Ontario, St. Lawrence River.*

www.waterfronttrail.org

To order your copy online, go to: www.lucidmap.ca/map-store/atlases/

Annual Great Waterfront Trail Adventure.

Celebrate the Great Lakes Waterfront Trail this summer with a multi-day biking adventure led by the Waterfront Regeneration Trust. Known for 'friends, finds, and fun', the Great Waterfront Trail Adventure is a popular annual summer event for many cyclists. Join us for this fully-supported, annual cycling holiday and feel the wind, water, and earth in a new way. Visit www.waterfronttrail.org for this year's itinerary and registration details including fund-raising options.

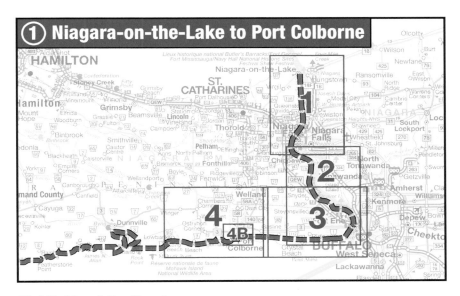

① Niagara-on-the-Lake to Port Colborne

Highlights of Section 1
A cornucopia of vineyards, wineries, historic forts and vibrant harbours. Visit WaterfrontTrail.org, NiagaraCycleTourism.com and OntarioByBike.ca for additional tourism information and trip plans.

Trail Runs Along:
Road shoulders and asphalt trail

Length: 142.6 Kilometres

Niagara-on-the-Lake to Port Colborne Map Pages

Map 1-1: Niagara-on-the-Lake
Map 1-2: Niagara Falls
Map 1-3: Fort Erie
Map 1-4: Port Colborne
Map 1-4A: Port Colborne - Detail

Fort Erie

Photos: Goh Iromoto

7

Map 1-1: Niagara-on-the-Lake

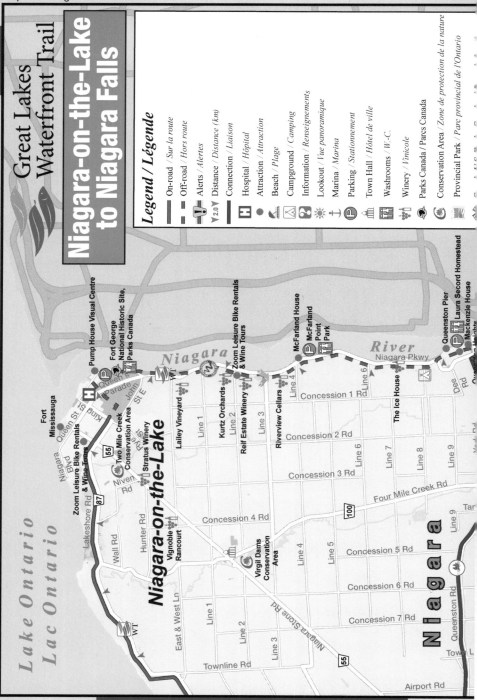

Great Lakes Waterfront Trail

Niagara-on-the-Lake to Niagara Falls

Legend / Légende

- On-road / Sur la route
- Off-road / Hors route
- Alerts / Alertes
- ▼2.0▼ Distance / Distance (km)
- Connection / Liaison
- Hospital / Hôpital
- Attraction / Attraction
- Beach / Plage
- Campground / Camping
- Information / Renseignements
- Lookout / Vue panoramique
- Marina / Marina
- Parking / Stationnement
- Town Hall / Hôtel de ville
- Washrooms / W.-C.
- Winery / Vinicole
- Parks Canada / Parcs Canada
- Conservation Area / Zone de protection de la nature
- Provincial Park / Parc provincial de l'Ontario

Map 1-1: Niagara Falls

Legend

- Canada-U.S. Border Crossing / *Poste de frontière*
- Trans Canada Trail / *Sentier Transcanadien*
- Greater Niagara Circle Route / *Route circulaire de la grande région de Niagara*
- Niagara River Recreational Trail / *Sentier d'excursion de la rivière Niagara*
- Greenbelt Route / *Sentier Greenbelt*
- Built-up / *Secteur bâti*
- Park, Natural Area / *Parc, Espace naturel*
- Marsh / *Marais*

New York U.S.A.

Niagara Falls

Scale

0 — 1 — 2 km

N

Lewiston-Queenston Bridge

Floral Clock

Lewiston-Queenston Bridge
No pedestrians, cyclists cross as a vehicle
Aucun piéton, les cyclistes traversent comme un vehicule

Mackenzie House

Queenston Heights Park

Steep hill with turns
Pente raide avec virages

Butterfly Conservatory
Botanical Gardens

Niagara Glen Nature Centre

Spanish Aero Car

White Water Walk

Zoom Leisure Bike Rentals & Wine Tours

Rainbow Bridge
Pedestrians permitted, cyclists cross as a vehicle
Piétons permis, les cyclistes traversent comme un vehicule

Rainbow Bridge

Canadian Midway

Maid of the Mist

Skylon Tower

Table Rock Scenic Tunnels

The Scow

Trail may be very busy
Le sentier pourrait être très passant

Niagara Falls

10,000 Buddha Temple

Sky Wheel

Niagara Falls Greenhouse & Mosaiculture Garden

Marineland

Ontario

Stanley Ave

Sinnicks Ave

Saint Paul Ave

Drummond Rd

Vincor

Greater Niagara General

Dorchester Rd

Riall St

O'Neil St

Tanbark Rd

General Brock Pkwy

Queen Elizabeth Way

Warner Rd

Mountain Rd

Kalar Rd

Montrose Rd

Woodbine St

Garner Rd

Thorold Stone Rd

Beaverdams Rd

Beechwood Rd

McLeod Rd

Brown Rd

Woodend Conservation Area

York Rd

Portage Rd

River Rd

Bridge St

Ferry St

Main St

Lundy's La

Portage Rd

McLeod Rd

Main St

Niagara Falls

La Rivière

Niagara Parkway

Welland River

9

Map 1-2: Niagara Falls

Great Lakes Waterfront Trail

Niagara Falls to Fort Erie

Map 1-2 Carte

Legend / Légende

- On-road / *Sur la route*
- Off-road / *Hors route*
- Alerts / *Alertes*
- ▼2.0▼ Distance / *Distance (km)*
- Connection / *Liaison*
- Hospital / *Hôpital*
- Attraction / *Attraction*
- Beach / *Plage*
- Campground / *Camping*
- Information / *Renseignements*
- Lookout / *Vue panoramique*
- Marina / *Marina*
- Parking / *Stationnement*
- Town Hall / *Hôtel de ville*
- Washrooms / *W.-C.*
- Winery / *Vinicole*
- Parks Canada / *Parcs Canada*
- Conservation Area / *Zone de protection de la nature*
- Provincial Park / *Parc provincial de l'Ontario*

Rainbow Bridge
Pedestrians permitted, cyclists cross as a vehicle
Aucun piéton, les cyclistes traversent comme un véhicule

9

New York
U.S.A.

Niagara Falls

Niagara River

River

Way

WT

Legends

Willoughby Historical Museum

Weaver Rd

Miller Rd

Niagara Pkwy

La

Willoughby Dr

Marshall Rd

Detenbeck Rd

Bossert Rd

Sherk Rd

Somerville Rd

Willick Rd

Sodom Rd

116

Ort Rd

Rainbow Bridge
Canadian Midway
Maid of the Mist
Skylon Tower
Sky Wheel
Table Rock Scenic Tunnels
The Scow

Greater Niagara General

McRae St
Ferry St
20
Main St
Dunn St
Drummond Rd
Lundy's La

Niagara Falls

Niagara Parks Greenhouses & Mosaiculture Garden

49

Portage Rd

Chippawa Pkwy

Main St

Marineland

Stanley Ave

102

Welland River

Lyons Creek Rd

Logan Rd

Stanley Ave

King Rd

47

Reixinger Rd

Beck Rd

Gonder Rd

Sauer Rd

QEW

River Rd

Map 1-2: Fort Erie

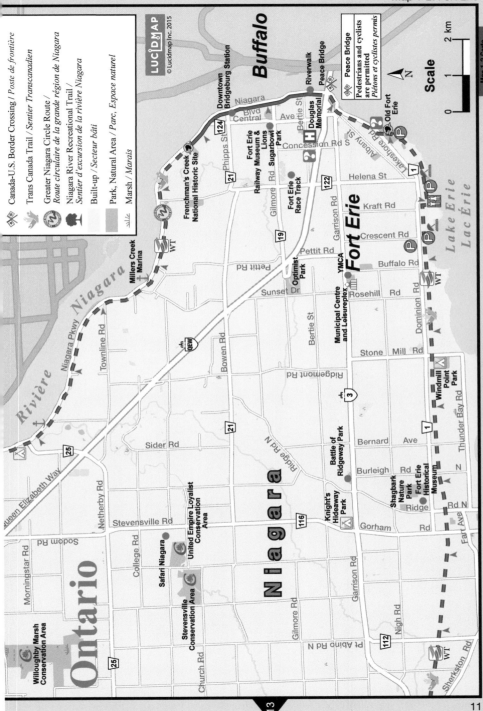

Map 1-2 Carte

Legend

- Canada-U.S. Border Crossing / *Poste de frontière*
- Trans Canada Trail / *Sentier Transcanadien*
- Greater Niagara Circle Route / *Route circulaire de la grande région de Niagara*
- Niagara River Recreational Trail / *Sentier d'excursion de la rivière Niagara*
- Built-up / *Secteur bâti*
- Park, Natural Area / *Parc, Espace naturel*
- Marsh / *Marais*

LUCIDMAP
© Lucidmap Inc. 2015

Scale

0   1   2 km

N

Peace Bridge
Pedestrians and cyclists are permitted
Piétons et cyclistes permis

Buffalo

Fort Erie

Ontario

Niagara

Lake Erie
Lac Érie

Niagara Pkwy

Rivière Niagara

Queen Elizabeth Way

Willoughby Marsh Conservation Area

Morningstar Rd

Sodom Rd

Netherby Rd

Stevensville Rd

College Rd

Church Rd

Sider Rd

Safari Niagara

Stevensville Conservation Area

United Empire Loyalist Conservation Area

Gilmore Rd

Ridge Rd N

Garrison Rd

Pt Abino Rd N

Knight's Hideaway Park

Battle of Ridgeway Park

Gorham Rd

Ridge Rd

Burleigh Rd

Bernard Ave

Shagbark Nature Park

Fort Erie Historical Museum

Nigh Rd

112

Sherkston Rd

Thunder Bay Rd

Windmill Point Park

Stone Mill Rd

Dominion Rd

Buffalo Rd

Crescent Rd

Kraft Rd

Helena St

Rosehill Rd

Municipal Centre and Leisureplex

YMCA

Optimist Park

Sunset Dr

Pettit Rd

Bowen Rd

Townline Rd

Ridgemont Rd

Bertie St

Garrison Rd

Millers Creek Marina

Frenchman's Creek National Historic Site

Phipps St

Niagara Blvd Central

Downtown Bridgeburg Station

Albany St

Bertie St

Concession Rd S

Douglas Memorial

Riverwalk

Peace Bridge

Old Fort Erie

Fort Erie Railway Museum & Lions Sugarbowl Park

Fort Erie Race Track

Lakeshore Rd

124

21

19

122

25

116

21

3

1

1

Map 1-3: Fort Erie

Map 1-3 Carte

Ridge Rd

Montrose Rd

Sodom Rd

Willoughby Marsh Conservation Area

25

Smith-Ness Forest Conservation Area

Netherby Rd, 25

Netherby Rd

Stevensville Rd

College Rd

Schih Rd

Forks Rd

Safari Niagara

Sider Rd

Church Rd

Stevensville Conservation Area

United Empire Loyalist Conservation Area

Brookfield Rd

Troup Rd

Neff Rd

98

Ontario
(Canada)

N i

Humberstone Marsh Conservation Area

Holloway Bay Rd

Gilmore Rd

Pt Abino Rd N

116

Ridge Rd N

2nd Conc Rd

Wilhelm Rd

Garrison Rd

Knight's Hideaway Park

Battle of Ridgeway P

15

112

Nigh Rd

Gorham

Burleigh Rd

Bernar

Ridgeway

Shagbark Nature Park

Ridge Rd N

Fort Erie Historical Museum

WT

Empire Rd

Beach

Sherkston Rd

WT

Farr Ave

Ridgeway Rd

S Pd N

Thur

Centennial Cedar Bay Park

Michener Rd

1

Crystal Beach

Bernar Pa

Sherkston Shores Park

Pleasant

Pt Abino Rd S

Erie Rd

Bay/Crystal Beach

Crystal Beach Waterfront Park & Boat Launch

Sherkston Beaches

N

Scale

0   1   2 km

Bertie Boating Club

Le

Point Abino Lighthouse

Great Lakes
Waterfront Trail

LUC[D]MAP

© Lucidmap Inc. 2015

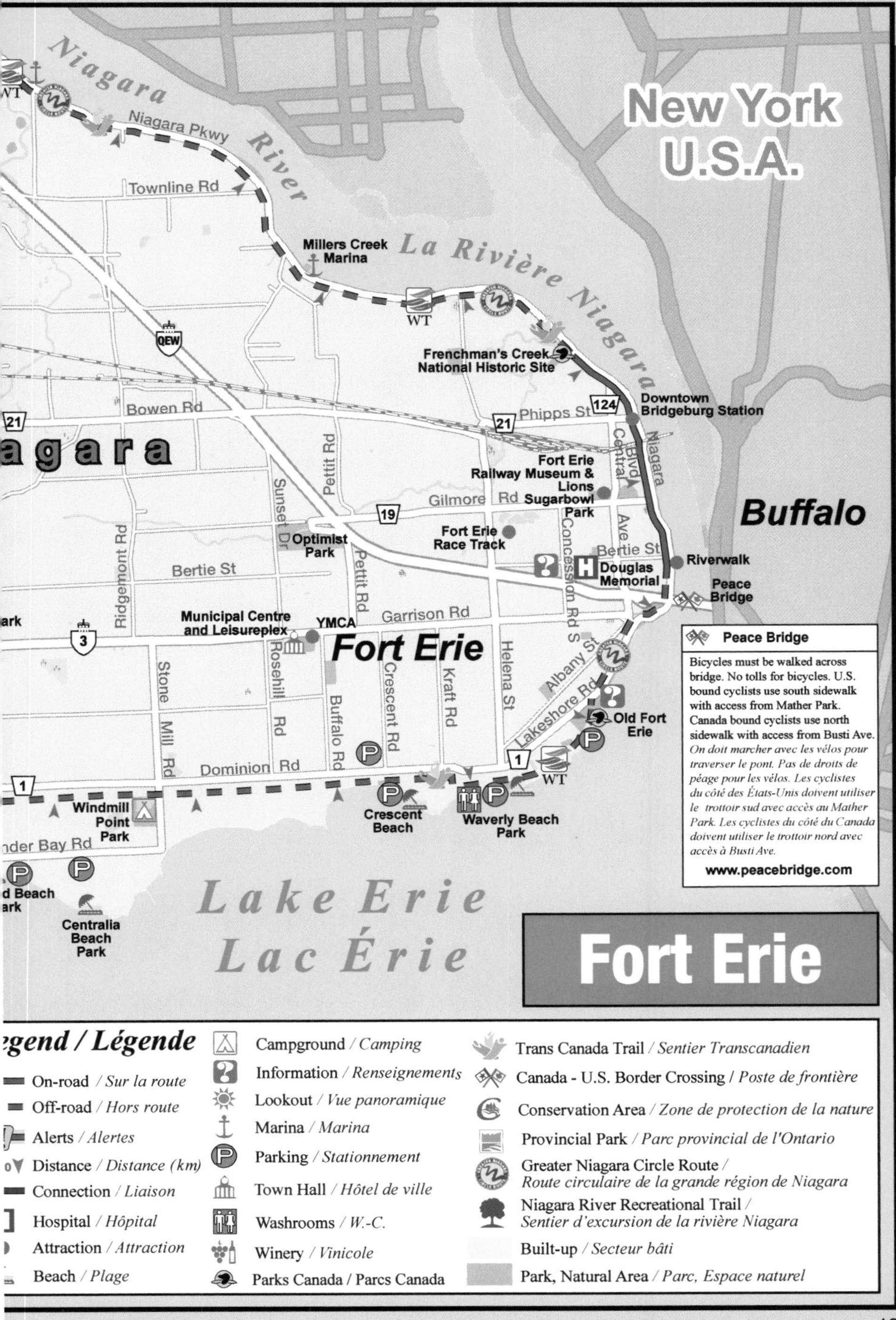
New York
U.S.A.
Niagara River
La Rivière Niagara
Niagara Pkwy
Townline Rd
Millers Creek
Marina
WT
QEW
Frenchman's Creek
National Historic Site
124
Downtown
Bridgeburg Station
Bowen Rd
21
Phipps St
agara
Central
Blvd
Niagara
Fort Erie
Railway Museum &
Lions
Sugarbowl
Park
Gilmore Rd
Pettit Rd
Sunset Dr
19
Buffalo
Optimist
Park
Fort Erie
Race Track
Concession Rd S
Ave
Bertie St
Riverwalk
Ridgemont Rd
Bertie St
Douglas
Memorial
Peace
Bridge
ark
Municipal Centre
and Leisureplex
YMCA
Garrison Rd
3
Fort Erie
Rosehill Rd
Stone Mill Rd
Buffalo Rd
Crescent Rd
Kraft Rd
Helena St
Albany St
Lakeshore Rd
Old Fort
Erie
Dominion Rd
1
Windmill
Point
Park
Crescent
Beach
Waverly Beach
Park
nder Bay Rd
d Beach
ark
Centralia
Beach
Park
Lake Erie
Lac Érie
Peace Bridge
Bicycles must be walked across bridge. No tolls for bicycles. U.S. bound cyclists use south sidewalk with access from Mather Park. Canada bound cyclists use north sidewalk with access from Busti Ave.
On doit marcher avec les vélos pour traverser le pont. Pas de droits de péage pour les vélos. Les cyclistes du côté des États-Unis doivent utiliser le trottoir sud avec accès au Mather Park. Les cyclistes du côté du Canada doivent utiliser le trottoir nord avec accès à Busti Ave.
www.peacebridge.com
Fort Erie
egend / Légende
On-road / Sur la route
Off-road / Hors route
Alerts / Alertes
Distance / Distance (km)
Connection / Liaison
Hospital / Hôpital
Attraction / Attraction
Beach / Plage
Campground / Camping
Information / Renseignements
Lookout / Vue panoramique
Marina / Marina
Parking / Stationnement
Town Hall / Hôtel de ville
Washrooms / W.-C.
Winery / Vinicole
Parks Canada / Parcs Canada
Trans Canada Trail / Sentier Transcanadien
Canada - U.S. Border Crossing / Poste de frontière
Conservation Area / Zone de protection de la nature
Provincial Park / Parc provincial de l'Ontario
Greater Niagara Circle Route / Route circulaire de la grande région de Niagara
Niagara River Recreational Trail / Sentier d'excursion de la rivière Niagara
Built-up / Secteur bâti
Park, Natural Area / Parc, Espace naturel

Map 1-4: Port Colborne

Map 1-4 Carte

Webber

Conc 6

27

E C Brown
Conservation Ar

Traver Rd

Smith Rd

Marr Rd

Winger Rd

Perry Rd

Putman Rd

Wilford Rd

24

Hewitt Rd

Ontario

Forks Rd

3

N i

Flanagan Rd

Sider Rd

Case Rd

Pettit Rd

Wilis Rd

Gilmore Rd

Bell Rd

Garringer Rd

Conc 2 Rd

Feeder Rd W

Sdrd 30

Sdrd 26

Sdrd 24

Sdrd 20

3

Dixie Rd

Outred Rd

Ditts Rd

21

65

Hutchinson Rd

Conc 1

Daley

Ditch Rd

3

Gord Harry Trail

Golf Course Rd

Burkett Rd

Long Beach
Conservation
Area

Brawn Rd

Station Rd

Burnaby Rd

3

N Shore Dr

Regional
Beach

Lakeshore Rd

WT

Harbourview Rd

WT

N

Scale

0   1   2 km

Lake Erie

Lac Érie

Morgan's Point
Conservation
Area

Legen

On-

Off-

Aler

2.0

Con

Con

H   Hos

Attr

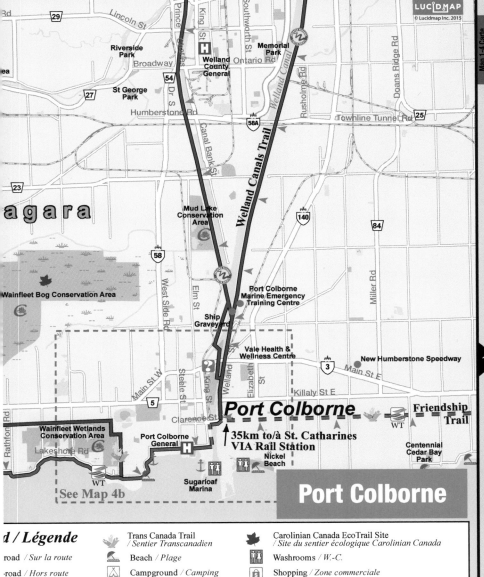

Map 1-4: Port Colborne

Port Colborne

35km to/à St. Catharines VIA Rail Station

See Map 4b

Légende / Legend

road / Sur la route	Trans Canada Trail / Sentier Transcanadien
-road / Hors route	Beach / Plage
rts / Alertes	Campground / Camping
ance / Distance (km)	Information / Renseignements
nection / Liaison	Lookout / Vue panoramique
nection / Liaison proposé	Marina / Marina
pital / Hôpital	Parking / Stationnement
action / Attraction	Town Hall / Hôtel de ville

Carolinian Canada EcoTrail Site / Site du sentier écologique Carolinian Canada
Washrooms / W.-C.
Shopping / Zone commerciale
Conservation Area / Zone de protection de la nature
Provincial Park / Parc provincial de l'Ontario
Built-up / Secteur bâti
Cemetery / Cimetière
Park, Natural Area / Parc, Espace naturel
Marsh / Marais

Map 1-4B: Port Colborne Detail Map

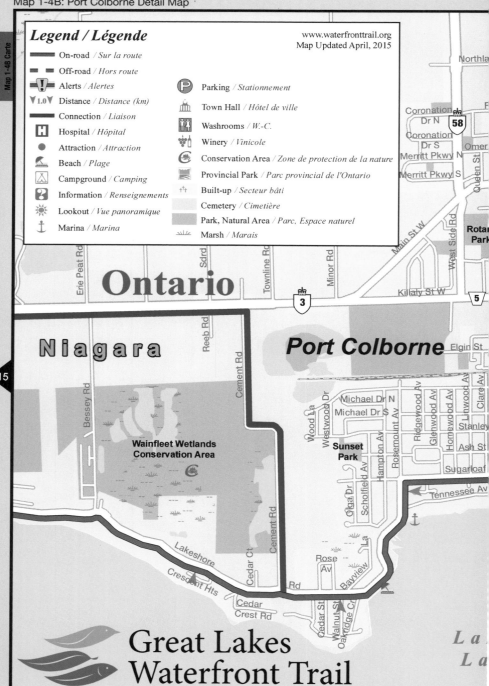

Map 1-4B Carte

Legend / Légende

www.waterfronttrail.org
Map Updated April, 2015

- On-road / *Sur la route*
- - - Off-road / *Hors route*
- Alerts / *Alertes*
- ▼1.0▼ Distance / *Distance (km)*
- Connection / *Liaison*
- **H** Hospital / *Hôpital*
- ● Attraction / *Attraction*
- Beach / *Plage*
- △ Campground / *Camping*
- **?** Information / *Renseignements*
- ☼ Lookout / *Vue panoramique*
- ⚓ Marina / *Marina*

- **P** Parking / *Stationnement*
- Town Hall / *Hôtel de ville*
- Washrooms / *W.-C.*
- Winery / *Vinicole*
- Conservation Area / *Zone de protection de la nature*
- Provincial Park / *Parc provincial de l'Ontario*
- ⊹ Built-up / *Secteur bâti*
- Cemetery / *Cimetière*
- Park, Natural Area / *Parc, Espace naturel*
- Marsh / *Marais*

Ontario

Niagara

Port Colborne

Wainfleet Wetlands
Conservation Area

Sunset
Park

Great Lakes
Waterfront Trail

16

Map 1-4B: Port Colborne Detail Map

Map 1-4B Carte

land Av

Royal Rd

Knoll St

Elm St

Franklin Av

Reservoir Park

Borden Av

Sherwood

Omer Av

er Av

Wallace Av

Main St W

Neff St

Neff St

George St

Highland Av

Vimy Park

McCain St

Elm St

ary rk

Knoll St

Steele St

Oakwood St

Silver St

Erie St

King St

Lions Field Park

Steele St

Elgin St

King St

Park St

Clarence St

Elm St

Forest Av

y St

Charlotte St

St

Kent St

Steele St

Alexandra St

Ash St

Port Colborne General

af St

Av

H H Knoll Lakeview Park

Marine Rd

Sugarloaf Marina

Derek Point La

Forest La

Weir Rd

Canal Rd

Bank Rd

Mellanby Av

Chippawa Rd

Derek Point Park

Berkley Av

Main St E

Chestnut St

Clarke St

John Av

Crescent Av

Janet St

Humboldt Pkwy

Wellington St

The Island

St

Canal Rd

Welland

Victoria St

Adelaide St

Welland St

Mitchell St

Davis St

Fares St

Lake Rd

King St

140

3

Vale Health & Wellness Centre

Killaly St E

Christmas St

Cross St

Bell St

Johnston St

Colborne St

Durham St

Davis St

Grassie Av

McRae Av

Fraser St

Lincoln Av

Mercury Av

James Av

| | Metal grate bridge |
| | *Pont en grillage métallique* |

15

Reuter Rd

Nickel Beach

N

Scale

0   0.5   1 km

ke Erie

ac Érie

Port Colborne

Haldimand County

Photo: Goh Iromoto

Norfolk County

Photo: Goh Iromoto

Waterfront Trail : Section 2

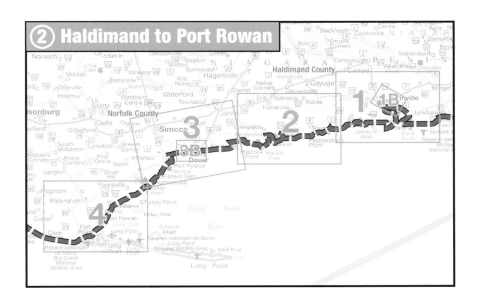

② Haldimand to Port Rowan

Highlights of Section 2
Lush farm fields, waterfront vistas, stunning beaches, protected natural areas, provincial parks, heritage rivers, wineries, ziplining and kayaking. Visit WaterfrontTrail.org, OntarioSouthwest.com and OntarioByBike.ca for additional tourism information and trip plans.

Trail Runs Along: Paved road shoulders
Length: 150 Kilometres

Haldimand to Port Rowan Map Pages
Map 2-1: Haldimand
Map 2-1B: Haldimand - Detail
Map 2-2: Rural Haldimand
Map 2-3: Norfolk
Map 2-3B: Port Dover - Detail
Map 2-4: Port Rowan

Map 2-1: Haldimand

Map 2-1 Carte

Ortt Rd

Junction Rd

Hald Dunn Townline Rd

Oakwood Escapes
Luxury Campground

James Rd

Moote Rd

15

Robinson Rd

River

Grand

River Rd

Haldimand War
Lions Memorial
Park Hospital

Du

Cedar St

Broad

Grand River
Marina

Byng Island
Conservation Area

Riverside
Marina

Port

Bains Road
Cider & Winery

Hald Dunn Townline Rd

Rainham Rd

Haldimand

Bains Rd

3

S Cayuga Rd

49

50

25

Johnson Rd

Kings Row

Yaremy Rd

Lakeshore

Rd

WT

Beach Rd

Marshall Rd

P

James N. Allan
Provincial Park

No bike lanes / Low traffic speeds
*Aucune chaussée désignée /
Faible vitesse de circulation*

Lighth

Sandy Bay Rd

N

Scale

0   1   2 km

Lake Erie
Lac Érie

Leg

2.0

H

Great Lakes
Waterfront Trail

LUC**I**D**MAP**

© Lucidmap Inc. 2015

Map 2-1: Haldimand

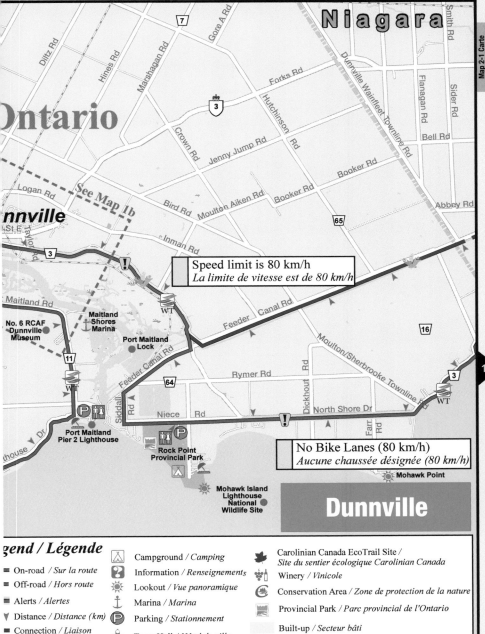

Niagara

Speed limit is 80 km/h
La limite de vitesse est de 80 km/h

No Bike Lanes (80 km/h)
Aucune chaussée désignée (80 km/h)

Mohawk Point

Dunnville

Mohawk Island
Lighthouse
National
Wildlife Site

Rock Point
Provincial Park

Port Maitland
Pier 2 Lighthouse

Niece Rd

Rymer Rd

North Shore Dr

Port Maitland
Lock

Feeder Canal Rd

Maitland
Shores
Marina

No. 6 RCAF
Dunnville
Museum

Maitland Rd

Inman Rd

See Map 1b

Ontario

Logan Rd

Bird Rd Moulton Aiken Rd Booker Rd Booker Rd

Jenny Jump Rd

Crown Rd

Hutchinson Rd

Forks Rd

Hines Rd

Ditz Rd

Marshagan Rd

Gore A Rd

Dunnville Wainfleet Townline Rd

Flanagan Rd

Sider Rd

Smith Rd

Bell Rd

Abbey Rd

Moulton/Sherbrooke Townline Rd

Dickhout Rd

Farr Rd

Siddall Rd

Feeder Canal Rd

7

3

65

16

3

14

11

64

3

Legend / Légende

▬ On-road / *Sur la route*	🏕 Campground / *Camping*
▬ Off-road / *Hors route*	❓ Information / *Renseignements*
▬ Alerts / *Alertes*	☀ Lookout / *Vue panoramique*
▼ Distance / *Distance (km)*	⚓ Marina / *Marina*
▬ Connection / *Liaison*	Ⓟ Parking / *Stationnement*
Hospital / *Hôpital*	🏛 Town Hall / *Hôtel de ville*
Attraction / *Attraction*	🚻 Washrooms / *W.-C.*
Beach / *Plage*	🦉 Bird Watching / *L'Observation des oiseaux*

Carolinian Canada EcoTrail Site /
Site du sentier écologique Carolinian Canada

🍇 Winery / *Vinicole*

🍁 Conservation Area / *Zone de protection de la nature*

Provincial Park / *Parc provincial de l'Ontario*

Built-up / *Secteur bâti*

✝ Cemetery / *Cimetière*

Park, Natural Area / *Parc, Espace naturel*

Marsh / *Marais*

Map 2-1 Carte

Map 2-1B: Dunnville Detail Map

Map 2-1B Carte

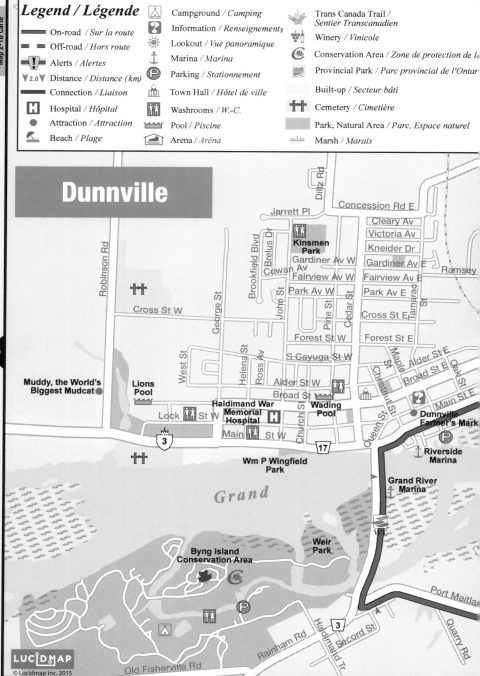

Legend / Légende

On-road / *Sur la route*	Campground / *Camping*	Trans Canada Trail / *Sentier Transcanadien*	
Off-road / *Hors route*	Information / *Renseignements*	Winery / *Vinicole*	
Alerts / *Alertes*	Lookout / *Vue panoramique*	Conservation Area / *Zone de protection de l*	
▼2.0▼ Distance / *Distance (km)*	Marina / *Marina*	Provincial Park / *Parc provincial de l'Ontar*	
Connection / *Liaison*	Parking / *Stationnement*	Built-up / *Secteur bâti*	
Hospital / *Hôpital*	Town Hall / *Hôtel de ville*	Cemetery / *Cimetière*	
Attraction / *Attraction*	Washrooms / *W.-C.*	Park, Natural Area / *Parc, Espace naturel*	
Beach / *Plage*	Pool / *Piscine*	Marsh / *Marais*	
	Arena / *Aréna*		

Dunnville

Jarrett Pl

Concession Rd E

Kinsmen Park

Cleary Av
Victoria Av
Kneider Dr

Dilz Rd

Robinson Rd

Brookfield Blvd
C Brelus Dr

Gardiner Av W
Cowan Av
Fairview Av W

Gardiner Av E
Ramsey
Fairview Av E

George St

John St

Park Av W
Pine St
Cedar St

Park Av E

Cross St W

Cross St E
Tamarac St

Forest St W

Forest St E

West St

Helena St
Ross Av

S Cayuga St W

Maple St

Alder St E
Chestnut St
Broad St E
Oak St

Muddy, the World's Biggest Mudcat ●

Lions Pool

Alder St W

Broad St W

Main St E

Haldimand War Memorial Hospital H

Wading Pool

Church St

Dunnville Farmer's Mark

Lock St W

Main St W

Queen St

Riverside Marina

3

17

Grand River Marina

Wm P Wingfield Park

Weir Park

We

Grand

Byng Island Conservation Area

Port Maitla

Rainham Rd

Haldimand Tr

Secord St

3

Quarry Rd

Old Fisherville Rd

20

Map 2-1B: Dunnville Detail Map

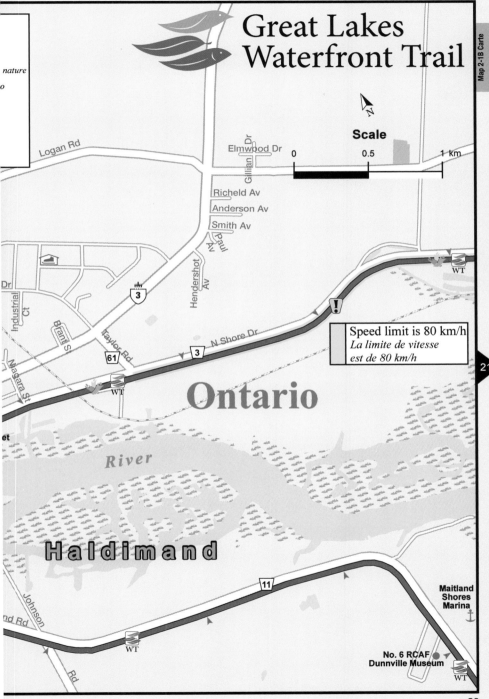

Great Lakes
Waterfront Trail

Map 2-1B Carte

N

Scale

0   0.5   1 km

nature

Logan Rd

Elmwood Dr

Gillian Dr

Richeld Av

Anderson Av

Smith Av

Paul Av

Hendershot Av

Dr

Industrial Ct

3

Brant St

Taylor Rd

61

3

N Shore Dr

Nagara St

WT

WT

Speed limit is 80 km/h
*La limite de vitesse
est de 80 km/h*

21

Ontario

River

Haldimand

Johnson

nd Rd

11

Maitland
Shores
Marina

WT

No. 6 RCAF
Dunnville Museum

WT

Rd

23

Map 2-2: Rural Haldimand

Map 2-2 Carte

Irish Ln

Conc 8 Walpole

Conc 7

Haldimand Rd 12

Talbot Rd

3

Ontario

Conc 6

12

Main St E

Conc 6 Walpole

Conc 5

Conc 5 Walpole

53

Walpole-Rainham Rd

Sandusk Rd

Conc 4 Walpole

18

Conc 3 Walpole

Cottonwood
Mansion
Museum

Gravel shoulder
Accotement en gravier

Erie St

Selkirk

Conc 2 Walpole

MacDonald School
Museum

Main St W

Community
Park

27

Rainham Rd

Selkirk Provincial
Park

Erie St S

Brooklin Rd

Wheeler Rd

3

Haldimand
Conservation
Area

Bluewater Pkwy

WT

WT

Lake

Nanticoke Thermal
Power Plant

Lac

N

Peacock
Point

Scale

0   1   2 km

**Great Lakes
Waterfront Trail**

LUCIDMAP
© Lucidmap Inc. 2015

Leg

2.0

H

24

Map 2-2: Rural Haldimand

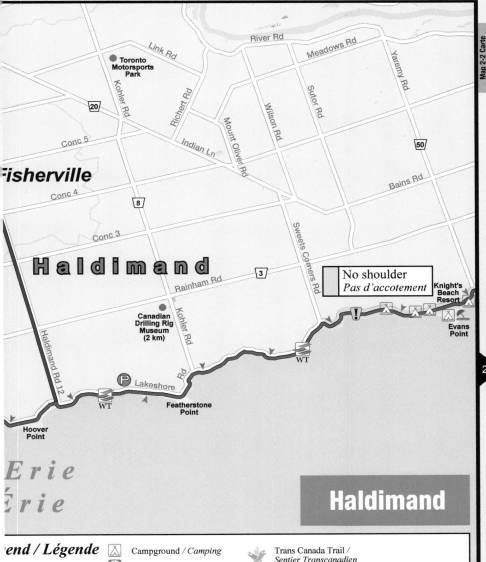

Haldimand

Map 2-2 Carte

end / Légende		
On-road / *Sur la route*	Campground / *Camping*	Trans Canada Trail / *Sentier Transcanadien*
Off-road / *Hors route*	Information / *Renseignements*	Winery / *Vinicole*
Alerts / *Alertes*	Lookout / *Vue panoramique*	Conservation Area / *Zone de protection de la nature*
Distance / *Distance (km)*	Marina / *Marina*	Provincial Park / *Parc provincial de l'Ontario*
Connection / *Liaison*	Parking / *Stationnement*	Built-up / *Secteur bâti*
Hospital / *Hôpital*	Town Hall / *Hôtel de ville*	Cemetery / *Cimetière*
Attraction / *Attraction*	Washrooms / *W.-C.*	Park, Natural Area / *Parc, Espace naturel*
Beach / *Plage*	Pool / *Piscine*	Marsh / *Marais*
	Arena / *Aréna*	

Map 2-3: Norfolk

Conc 14

Sutton
Conservation
Area

[24]

[3]

On

Conc 6

Blue Line

Rd

Mcdowell Rd E

Hillcrest Rd

Simcoe

Brook
Conservation
Area

Decou Rd

Ireland Rd

Conc 5

Charlotteville Rd 8

Charlotteville Rd 7

Lynn Valley Rd

Charlotteville Rd 5

Saint Johns Rd E

Lynn Valley Trail
44 km to/ à Brantford
VIA Rail Station

[3]

Saint Johns Rd W

Hillcrest Rd S

[3]

Charlotteville East Quarter Line Rd

Charlotteville Rd 5

Port Ryerse Rd

Blue Line Rd

HWY
[6]

Main St

St. George

31

Old Brock St

Vittoria Rd

[24]
HWY

Radical Rd

Nelson St N

Vittoria / Sowden
Conservation
Area

Hay Creek
Conservation Area

See Map 3b

[57]

Kitchen Rd

Incline
Montée

Charlotteville Rd 2

Norfolk

Front Rd

Commercial
Rd

HWY
[24]

Fishers Glen Rd

Lake Erie
Lac Érie

Norfolk
Conservation Area

Fishers Glen
Conservation
Area

WT

Front Rd

Incline
Montée

Incline
Montée

Leg

Turkey Point
Provincial Park

Incline
Montée

Steep Hill
Pente escarpée

▼2.0

H

Port Dover

Map 2-3 Carte

Map 2-3: Norfolk

Map 2-3 Carte

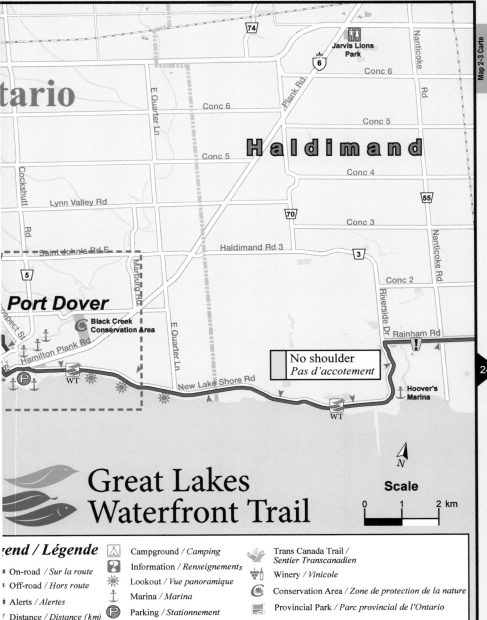

Great Lakes
Waterfront Trail

Scale

0   1   2 km

No shoulder
Pas d'accotement

Legend / Légende

- On-road / *Sur la route*
- Off-road / *Hors route*
- Alerts / *Alertes*
- Distance / *Distance (km)*
- Connection / *Liaison*
- Hospital / *Hôpital*
- Attraction / *Attraction*
- Beach / *Plage*

- Campground / *Camping*
- Information / *Renseignements*
- Lookout / *Vue panoramique*
- Marina / *Marina*
- Parking / *Stationnement*
- Town Hall / *Hôtel de ville*
- Washrooms / *W.-C.*
- Pool / *Piscine*
- Arena / *Aréna*

- Trans Canada Trail / *Sentier Transcanadien*
- Winery / *Vinicole*
- Conservation Area / *Zone de protection de la nature*
- Provincial Park / *Parc provincial de l'Ontario*
- Built-up / *Secteur bâti*
- Cemetery / *Cimetière*
- Park, Natural Area / *Parc, Espace naturel*
- Marsh / *Marais*

Map 2-3B: Port Dover Detail Map

Map 2-3B Carte

Saint John's Rd E

Ontario

Lynn Valley Trail
**44 km to/à Brantford
VIA Rail Station**

Tisdale Rd

Kelly Dr

Lynn Park Av

Dover Mills

Prospect St

Birch

Blue Lake Av

Main St

Saint George St

HWY **6**

Dover Av

Silver

Greenock St E

26

Richardson Dr

Greenock St W

1st Av

Saint George St

Main St

Saint Andrew St

Saint Patric

B

Port Dover

Mergl Dr

Regent Av

Saint George St

**Lighthouse
Festival
Theatre**

WT

H

Blue Line Rd

Nelson St W

Cumberland St

WT

N

Scale

| 0 | 0.5 | 1 km |

Great Lakes
Waterfront Trail

LUC**i**DMAP
© Lucidmap Inc. 2015

Leg

▼2.0▼

H

28

Map 2-3B: Port Dover Detail Map

Map 2-3B Carte

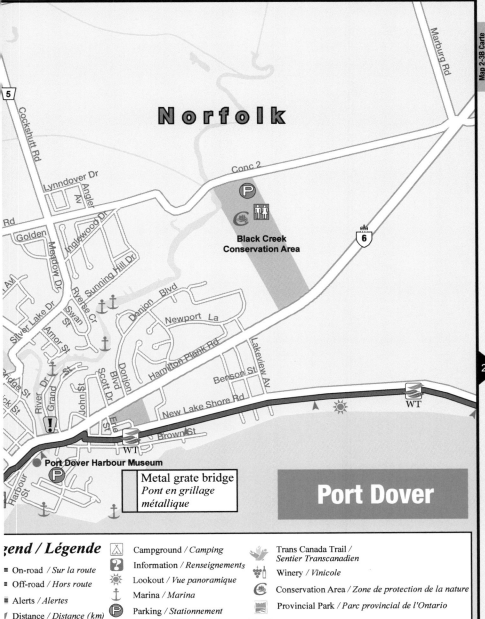

Norfolk

Conc 2

**Black Creek
Conservation Area**

5

6

Cockshutt Rd

Lynndover Dr

Angler Av

Golden

Meadow Dr

Inglewood Dr

Sunning Hill Dr

Silver Lake Dr

Ryerse Cr

Swan St

Amor St

Donion Blvd

Newport La

Hamilton Plank Rd

Lakeview Av

Benson St

Bridge St

River Dr

Grand St

John's St

Scott Dr

Donion Blvd

Erie St

New Lake Shore Rd

Brown St

WT

WT

27

Port Dover Harbour Museum

| Metal grate bridge |
| *Pont en grillage* |
| *métallique* |

Port Dover

Harbour St

---

gend / Légende

Campground / *Camping*

Trans Canada Trail / *Sentier Transcanadien*

■ On-road / *Sur la route*

Information / *Renseignements*

Winery / *Vinicole*

■ Off-road / *Hors route*

Lookout / *Vue panoramique*

Conservation Area / *Zone de protection de la nature*

■ Alerts / *Alertes*

Marina / *Marina*

Provincial Park / *Parc provincial de l'Ontario*

Distance / *Distance (km)*

Parking / *Stationnement*

■ Connection / *Liaison*

Town Hall / *Hôtel de ville*

Built-up / *Secteur bâti*

Hospital / *Hôpital*

Washrooms / *W.-C.*

Cemetery / *Cimetière*

Attraction / *Attraction*

Pool / *Piscine*

Park, Natural Area / *Parc, Espace naturel*

Beach / *Plage*

Arena / *Aréna*

Marsh / *Marais*

Map 2-4: Port Rowan

Map 2-4 Carte

Port Rowan

E Quarter Line Rd

E Quarter Line R

Lakeshore Rd

1st Conc Rd

Carolina Way

Aspen La

Bay St

Erie Av

Price St

Wolven St

Front Rd

6th Conc Rd

60

On

Dedrick Rd

Hunter Dr N

College Av

Front Rd

Dock St

Historical Plaque

HWY 59

Backus Conser

WT

Lakeshore Rd

WT

0   0.5   1 km

Cultus Rd

3rd Conc Rd

2nd Conc Rd

Po

7th Conc Rd

23

Rowan Mills Conservation Area

6th Conc Rd

1st Conc Rd

Norfolk

Big

Lakesh

Conc A

Lee Brown Waterfo Management Area

WT

42

Lakeshore Rd

WT

Port Rowan

Great Lakes
Waterfront Trail

N

Scale

0   1   2 km

Leg

!

2.0

H

35

Map 2-4: Port Rowan

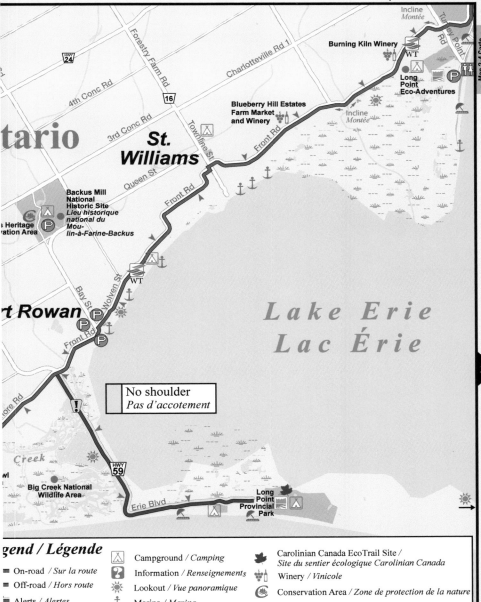

Incline
Montée

Burning Kiln Winery
WT

Long
Point
Eco-Adventures

Charlotteville Rd 1

Forestry Farm Rd

16

Blueberry Hill Estates
Farm Market
and Winery

Incline
Montée

Front Rd

tario

St. Williams

3rd Conc Rd

4th Conc Rd

Queen St

Townline St

Front Rd

Backus Mill
National
Historic Site
*Lieu historique
national du
Mou-
lin-à-Farine-Backus*

s Heritage
ation Area

Bay St

Wolven St

WT

t Rowan

Front Rd

Lake Erie
Lac Érie

26

| No shoulder |
| *Pas d'accotement* |

ore Rd

Creek

wl

HWY
59

Big Creek National
Wildlife Area

Erie Blvd

Long
Point
Provincial
Park

---

gend / *Légende*

- On-road / *Sur la route*
- Off-road / *Hors route*
- Alerts / *Alertes*
- ▼ Distance / *Distance (km)*
- Connection / *Liaison*
- | Hospital / *Hôpital*
- Attraction / *Attraction*
- Beach / *Plage*

⚐ Campground / *Camping*
❓ Information / *Renseignements*
☀ Lookout / *Vue panoramique*
⚓ Marina / *Marina*
Ⓟ Parking / *Stationnement*
🏛 Town Hall / *Hôtel de ville*
🚻 Washrooms / *W.-C.*
🐦 Bird Watching /
L'Observation des oiseaux

🍁 Carolinian Canada EcoTrail Site /
Site du sentier écologique Carolinian Canada
🍇 Winery / *Vinicole*
Ⓖ Conservation Area / *Zone de protection de la nature*
▦ Provincial Park / *Parc provincial de l'Ontario*
Built-up / *Secteur bâti*
✝✝ Cemetery / *Cimetière*
Park, Natural Area / *Parc, Espace naturel*
Marsh / *Marais*

Port Stanley

Photo: Goh Iromoto

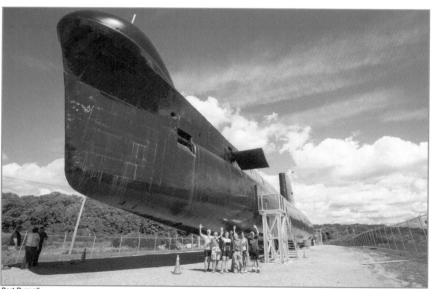

Port Burwell

Photo: Goh Iromoto

Waterfront Trail : Section 3

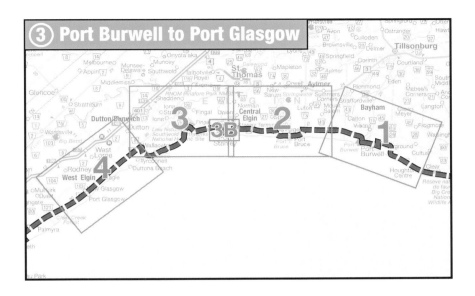

Highlights of Section 3

A glimpse of yesterday in scenic fishing hamlets where you can order fresh perch from any diner and stroll along expanses of beautiful beaches. Great night-life, eating and shopping in Port Stanley and an opportunity to tour a nuclear submarine from the cold-war era in Port Burwell. Visit WaterfrontTrail.org, OntarioSouthwest.com and OntarioByBike.ca for additional tourism information and trip plans.

Trail Runs Along: Paved roads on shoulders. Some short gravel sections.
Length: 126.95 Kilometres

Port Burwell to Port Glasgow Map Pages
Map 3-1: Port Burwell
Map 3-2: Elgin
Map 3-3: Port Stanley
Map 3-3B: Port Stanley - Detail
Map 3-4: Port Glasgow

Map 3-1: Port Burwell

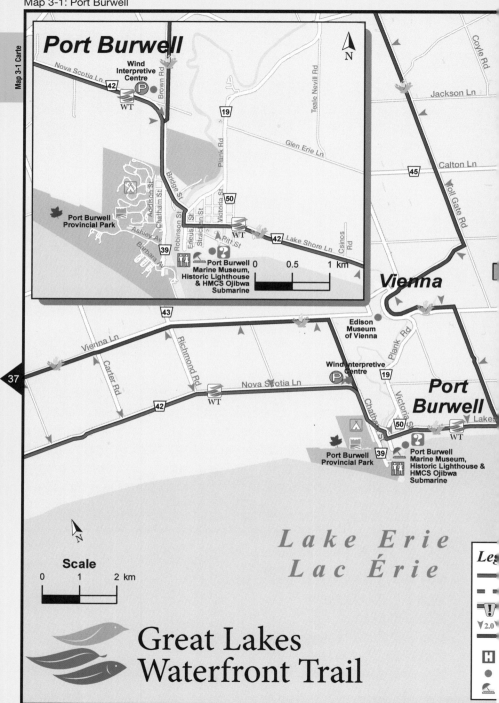

Port Burwell

Port Burwell
Provincial Park

Port Burwell
Marine Museum,
Historic Lighthouse
& HMCS Ojibwa
Submarine

Vienna

Edison
Museum
of Vienna

Wind Interpretive
Centre

Port
Burwell

Port Burwell
Provincial Park

Port Burwell
Marine Museum,
Historic Lighthouse &
HMCS Ojibwa
Submarine

Lake Erie
Lac Érie

Scale
0   1   2 km

Great Lakes
Waterfront Trail

Leg

▼2.0

Map 3-1: Port Burwell

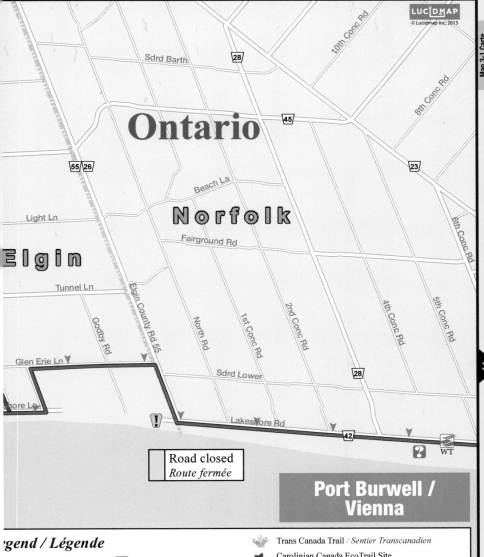

Map 3-1 Carte

Ontario

Norfolk

Elgin

Sdrd Barth

10th Conc Rd

8th Conc Rd

Beach La

Light Ln

Fairground Rd

Tunnel Ln

Elgin County Rd 55

Godby Rd

North Rd

1st Conc Rd

2nd Conc Rd

4th Conc Rd

5th Conc Rd

8th Conc Rd

Glen Erie Ln

Sdrd Lower

Lakeshore Rd

30

WT

| Road closed |
| Route fermée |

Port Burwell / Vienna

Legend / Légende

▬ On-road / *Sur la route*	🏕 Campground / *Camping*
▬ Off-road / *Hors route*	❓ Information / *Renseignements*
⌐ Alerts / *Alertes*	☼ Lookout / *Vue panoramique*
Distance / *Distance (km)*	⚓ Marina / *Marina*
▬ Connection / *Liaison*	Ⓟ Parking / *Stationnement*
Hospital / *Hôpital*	🏛 Town Hall / *Hôtel de ville*
Attraction / *Attraction*	🚻 Washrooms / *W.-C.*
Beach / *Plage*	

🌿 Trans Canada Trail / *Sentier Transcanadien*	
🍁 Carolinian Canada EcoTrail Site / *Site du sentier écologique Carolinian Canada*	
🍷 Winery / *Vinicole*	
Ⓖ Conservation Area / *Zone de protection de la nature*	
Provincial Park / *Parc provincial de l'Ontario*	
Built-up / *Secteur bâti*	
Cemetery / *Cimetière*	
Park, Natural Area / *Parc, Espace naturel*	
Marsh / *Marais*	

Map 3-2: Elgin

Map 3-2 Carte

St. Thomas

St. Thomas Elgin
General Hospital

40 km to/à London VIA Rail Station

Elm St   Elm Ln

56

36

Arc
Conse

28

Southdale Ln

Centennial Rd

John Wise Ln

45

Ontario

Fairview Rd

4

Fruit Ridge Ln

22

Quai Du Vin
Winery

Sparta Ln

Sunset Rd

Sunset Dr

Wilson Av

5th Av

st Av

YarmouttCentre Rd

Paved shoulder to St. Thomas
Accotements pavés vers Saint-Thomas

Quaker Rd

Roberts Ln

Gravel road
Route en gravier

39

East Rd

Dexter Ln

WT   24

YarmouttCentre Rd

36

Hawk Cliff Rd

Hawk Cliff Wildlife Area

Barnums Gully Ln

N

Lake Erie
Lac Érie

Scale
0   1   2 km

Legen

Or
Of
Al
2.0 Di
Co
Co
H Ho
At

Great Lakes
Waterfront Trail

Map 3-2: Elgin

Map 3-2 Carte

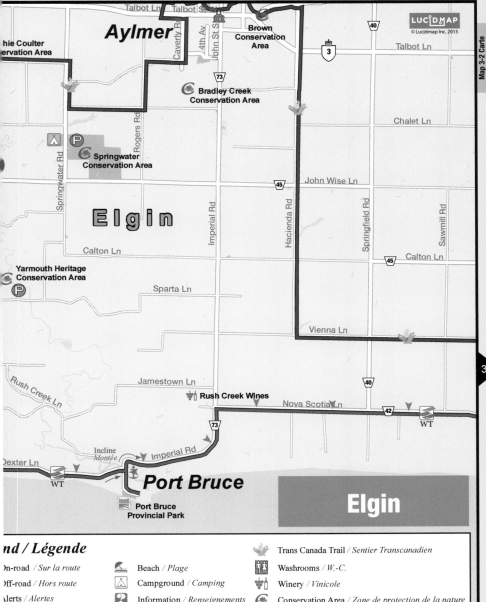

Aylmer

Brown Conservation Area

hie Coulter
ervation Area

Talbot Ln

Talbot St

Bradley Creek Conservation Area

Chalet Ln

Springwater Conservation Area

Elgin

John Wise Ln

Calton Ln

Yarmouth Heritage Conservation Area

Sparta Ln

Calton Ln

Vienna Ln

Jamestown Ln

Rush Creek Wines

Nova Scotia Ln

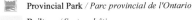

WT

Incline
Montée

Imperial Rd

Dexter Ln

WT

Port Bruce

Port Bruce Provincial Park

Elgin

Talbot Ln, 4th Av, John St St, Caverly Rd, Rogers Rd, Springwater Rd, Imperial Rd, Hacienda Rd, Springfield Rd, Sawmill Rd, Rush Creek Ln, Dexter Ln

---

nd / Légende

)n-road / *Sur la route*	Beach / *Plage*	Washrooms / *W.-C.*	Trans Canada Trail / *Sentier Transcanadien*
)ff-road / *Hors route*	⬚ Campground / *Camping*	Winery / *Vinicole*	
lerts / *Alertes*	? Information / *Renseignements*	Conservation Area / *Zone de protection de la nature*	
)istance / *Distance (km)*	☼ Lookout / *Vue panoramique*	Provincial Park / *Parc provincial de l'Ontario*	
:onnection / *Liaison*	⚓ Marina / *Marina*	Built-up / *Secteur bâti*	
:onnection / *Liaison proposé*	Ⓟ Parking / *Stationnement*	Cemetery / *Cimetière*	
lospital / *Hôpital*	🏛 Town Hall / *Hôtel de ville*	Park, Natural Area / *Parc, Espace naturel*	
.ttraction / *Attraction*		Marsh / *Marais*	

Map 3-3: Port Stanley

Map 3-3 Carte

Aberdeen Ln

Gore 5th Ln

Lawrence Rd

Moore Rd

6th Ln

Talbot Ln

3

401

Iona Rd

Shackleton Ln

Thomson Ln

Homestead Rd

Iona Rd

Onta

Southwold
Earthworks
National
Historic
Site

14

*Lieu historique
national des
Remblais-de-Southwold*

Elgin

Silver Clay Ln

Talbot Ln

Willey Rd

43

8

Currie Rd

3

Walnut Ln

Erin Ln

Incline
Montée

WT

Fingal Ln

16

WT

Ash Ln

Docker Rd

Lake View Ln

Plum Point Rd

Loose surface road
Route en gravier

Coyne Rd

N

**John E. Pearce
Provincial Park**

Scale

0   1   2 km

Great Lakes
Waterfront Trail

Leg

2.0

H

Map 3-3: Port Stanley

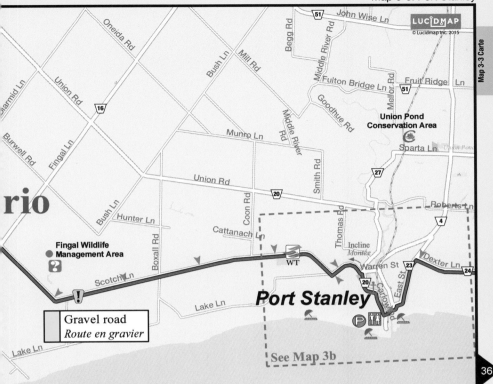

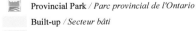

Port Stanley

Lake Erie
Lac Érie

Port Stanley

gend / Légende

▬	On-road / *Sur la route*	🗒	Campground / *Camping*	🍇	Winery / *Vinicole*	
▬	Off-road / *Hors route*	❓	Information / *Renseignements*	🌿	Conservation Area / *Zone de protection de la nature*	
▬	Alerts / *Alertes*	☀	Lookout / *Vue panoramique*	🏞	Provincial Park / *Parc provincial de l'Ontario*	
Ⅴ	Distance / *Distance (km)*	⚓	Marina / *Marina*		Built-up / *Secteur bâti*	
▬	Connection / *Liaison*	Ⓟ	Parking / *Stationnement*	✝	Cemetery / *Cimetière*	
▮	Hospital / *Hôpital*	🏛	Town Hall / *Hôtel de ville*		Park, Natural Area / *Parc, Espace naturel*	
	Attraction / *Attraction*	🚻	Washrooms / *W.-C.*	〰	Marsh / *Marais*	
	Beach / *Plage*					

Map 3-3B: Port Stanley Detail Map

LUC**i**DMAP
© Lucidmap Inc. 2015

Map 3-3B Carte

Ontario

Elgin

27

Union Rd

Thomas Rd

WT

Scotch Ln

Lake Ln

Incline
Montée

Warren St

21

Catherine St

Stanley St

Elizabeth St

Lake Ln

Port Stanley

20

WT

Carlow

39

George St

Spring St

Walnut St

Valley St

W Edith

Cavell Blvd

Front St

Smith St

Erie St

P

1st St

Edith Cavell Blvd

William St

N

Scale

0   0.5   1 km

Lake Erie
Lac Érie

Great Lakes
Waterfront Trail

Leg

▼1.0

H

●

Map 3-3B: Port Stanley Detail Map

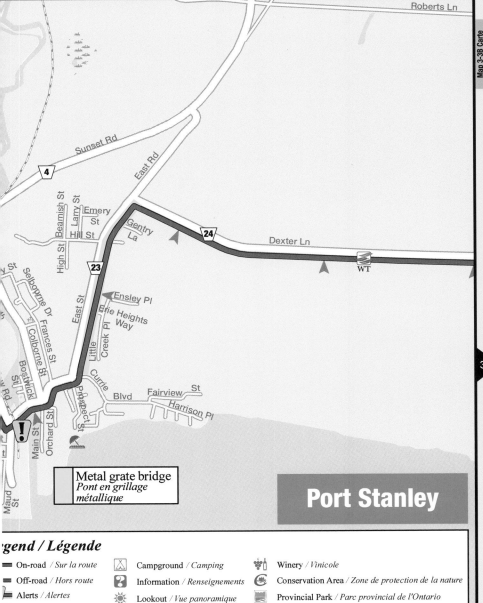

Roberts Ln

Map 3-3B Carte

Sunset Rd

East Rd

4

Beamish St

Larry St

Emery St

Hill St

Gentry La

24

Dexter Ln

WT

High St

23

Ensley Pl

Erie Heights Way

Selbourne Dr

Frances St

Colborne St

East St

Little Creek Pl

39

Bostwick St

Currie Blvd

Fairview St

Harrison Pl

Prospect St

Orchard St

Main St

Maud St

Metal grate bridge
Pont en grillage métallique

Port Stanley

On-road / *Sur la route*	Campground / *Camping*	Winery / *Vinicole*
Off-road / *Hors route*	Information / *Renseignements*	Conservation Area / *Zone de protection de la nature*
Alerts / *Alertes*	Lookout / *Vue panoramique*	Provincial Park / *Parc provincial de l'Ontario*
Distance / *Distance (km)*	Marina / *Marina*	Built-up / *Secteur bâti*
Connection / *Liaison*	Parking / *Stationnement*	Cemetery / *Cimetière*
Hospital / *Hôpital*	Town Hall / *Hôtel de ville*	Park, Natural Area / *Parc, Espace naturel*
Attraction / *Attraction*	Washrooms / *W.-C.*	Marsh / *Marais*
Beach / *Plage*		

Map 3-4: Port Glasgow

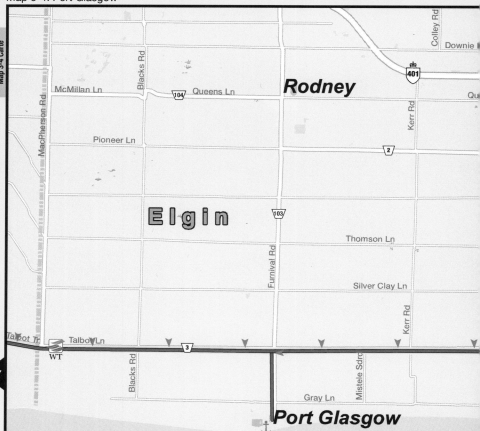

Rodney

Elgin

Thomson Ln

Silver Clay Ln

Port Glasgow

Lake Er
Lac Ér

West Lorne

Legend / Légende

On-road / *Sur la route*	
Off-road / *Hors route*	
Alerts / *Alertes*	
▼2.0▼ Distance / *Distance (km)*	
Connection / *Liaison*	
H Hospital / *Hôpital*	
● Attraction / *Attraction*	
Beach / *Plage*	

Campground / *Camping*	
Information / *Renseignements*	
Lookout / *Vue panoramique*	
Marina / *Marina*	
P Parking / *Stationnement*	
Town Hall / *Hôtel de ville*	
Washrooms / *W.-C.*	

Carolinian Canada EcoTrail Site / *Site du sentier écologique Carolinian Canada*	
Winery / *Vinicole*	
Conservation Area / *Zone de protection de la nat*	
Provincial Park / *Parc provincial de l'Ontario*	
Built-up / *Secteur bâti*	
Cemetery / *Cimetière*	
Park, Natural Area / *Parc, Espace naturel*	
Marsh / *Marais*	

Map 3-4: Port Glasgow

Chatham-Kent

Photo: Goh Iromoto

Chatham-Kent

Photo: Goh Iromoto

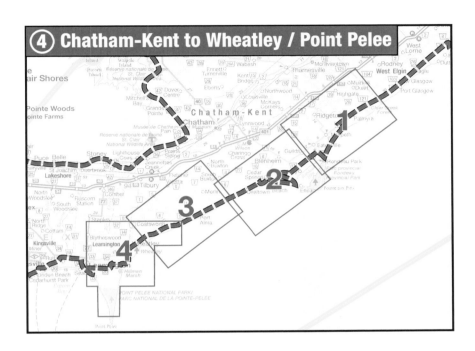

Highlights of Section 4

Acres of green farm fields dotted by 100+ wind turbines, beach hamlets with craft breweries and great diners, verdant provincial parks and Point Pelee National Park – southern most point in mainland Canada. Visit WaterfrontTrail.org, OntarioSouthwest.com and OntarioByBike.ca for additional tourism information and trip plans.

Trail Runs Along: Rural roads with paved shoulders and a 36 km stretch on gravel roads
Length: 128.6 Kilometres

Chatham-Kent to Wheatley / Point Pelee Map Pages
Map 4-1: Chatham-Kent
Map 4-2: Erieau
Map 4-3: Rural Chatham-Kent
Map 4-4: Wheatley / Point Pelee

Map 4-1: Chatham-Kent

Map 4-1 Carte

Welch Ln

Cotell

Mitton Ln

Colby Rd

Victoria Rd

Gosnell Ln

Base Rd

Ridgetown

Ree

19

Ridge Ln

Main St W

Erie St N

Erie St S

Holdaway Ln

Kent Bridge Rd

Shewburg Rd

Scane Rd

Moore Rd

Golf Cou

Chatha

Brush Ln

Green Ln

Ontario

Front Ln

Klondyke Ln

McKinlay Rd

17

Historic
Morpeth
Cemetery

Incline
Montée

Desmond Rd

Ed's Ln

Morpeth ✞✞

3

Talbot Tr

Greenview
Aviaries
Park & Zoo

Taylor Rd

Incline
Montée

G
h
A
à

Sinclair Ln

15

Antrim Rd

Hill Rd

Incline
Montée

Rondeau Shores
Trailer Park

New Scotland Ln

11

WT

Wildwood
Trailer Park

Terrace
Beach

49

Rose Beach Ln

No shoulders (60 km/hr)
Pas d'accotement (60 km/hr)

Rondeau
Provincial Park

Lake Erie
Lac Érie

Great Lakes
Waterfront Trail

Leg

▼2.0

H

LUC**I**DMAP
© Lucidmap Inc. 2015

Map 4-1: Chatham-Kent

Map 4-1 Carte

Highgate

Braemore Ln
Hastings Ln
Gillis Ln
Goodbrand Ln
Mazan Ln
King St
Duart Rd
19
Scott Ln
ders Ln
Muirkirk Ln
19
McLean Ln
rse Ln
20
Gesner Ln
m - K e n t
Tower Rd
Bury Rd
Teetzel Ln
Schweitzer Ln
Cleeves Ln
Thomson Ln
Kress Rd
Cleeves Ln
121
Eberle Ln
McDonald Ln
Kenesserie Rd
Cochrane Ln
Historic
Palmyra
Cemetery
Palmyra Rd
Crazy 8
Barn
Bury Rd
Morrison Rd
Clear Creek Forest
Provincial
Nature Reserve
WT
Talbot Tr
3
ravel shoulders,
igh speed traffic (90 km/hr)
ccotement gravier, circulation
haute vitesse (90 km/h)
WT
Bury
Cemetery
42
Clearville Rd
Clearville Park
Campground

Scale

0   1   2 km

Ridgetown /
Highgate

gend / Légende

- On-road / *Sur la route*
- Off-road / *Hors route*
- Alerts / *Alertes*
▼ Distance / *Distance (km)*
- Connection / *Liaison*
| Hospital / *Hôpital*
Attraction / *Attraction*
Beach / *Plage*

⬡ Campground / *Camping*
❓ Information / *Renseignements*
☼ Lookout / *Vue panoramique*
⚓ Marina / *Marina*
Ⓟ Parking / *Stationnement*
🏛 Town Hall / *Hôtel de ville*
🚻 Washrooms / *W.-C.*
👓 Bird Watching /
L'Observation des oiseaux

🍁 Carolinian Canada EcoTrail Site /
Site du sentier écologique Carolinian Canada
🍇 Winery / *Vinicole*
Ⓖ Conservation Area / *Zone de protection de la nature*
Provincial Park / *Parc provincial de l'Ontario*
Built-up / *Secteur bâti*
✝✝ Cemetery / *Cimetière*
Park, Natural Area / *Parc, Espace naturel*
⚶ Marsh / *Marais*

Map 4-2: Erieau

Map 4-2 Carte

13th Ln

16 km to Buxton Museum celebrating the Underground Railway and Early Black setttlements.

14th Ln

Drake Rd

A D Shadd Rd

Bloomfield Rd

Ontario

6

27

WT

15th Ln

Goulet Rd

Four Rod Rd

Charing Cross Rd

Gravel Road
Route en gravier

16th Ln

3

Dillon Rd

Talbot Tr

17th Ln

20 km to/à Cha
VIA Rail Sta

10

Craford Rd

Delhaven
Fruit Stand

Water St

Craford Historic
Cemetery

Douglas
Rd

51

↗N

Lake Erie
Lac Érie

Scale

0   1   2 km

Sharp Turr
*Tournant br
virage pron*

Great Lakes
Waterfront Trail

Legend / Légende

—— On-road / *Sur la route*
– – – Off-road / *Hors route*
⚠ Alerts / *Alertes*
▼2.0▼ Distance / *Distance (km)*
—— Connection / *Liaison*
🅷 Hospital / *Hôpital*
● Attraction / *Attraction*
⚓ Beach / *Plage*

⛺ Campground / *Camping*
ℹ Information / *Renseignements*
☀ Lookout / *Vue panoramique*
⚓ Marina / *Marina*
🅿 Parking / *Stationnement*
🏛 Town Hall / *Hôtel de ville*
🚻 Washrooms / *W.-C.*
🐦 Bird Watching /
   L'Observation des oiseaux

🍂 Carolinian Canada EcoTrail Site /
   Site du sentier écologique Carolinian Canada
🍇 Winery / *Vinicole*
Ⓒ Conservation Area / *Zone de protection de la*
▬ Provincial Park / *Parc provincial de l'Ontario*
Built-up / *Secteur bâti*
✝✝ Cemetery / *Cimetière*
Park, Natural Area / *Parc, Espace naturel*
⌇ Marsh / *Marais*

Map 4-2: Erieau

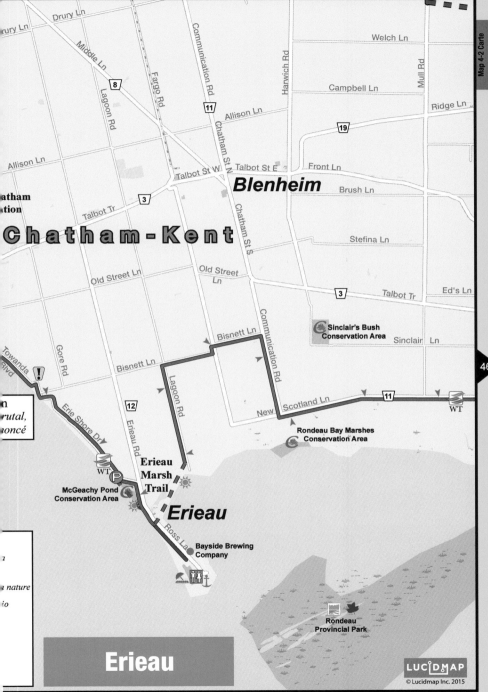

Blenheim

Chatham-Kent

Erieau
Marsh
Trail

Erieau

McGeachy Pond
Conservation Area

Sinclair's Bush
Conservation Area

Rondeau Bay Marshes
Conservation Area

Bayside Brewing
Company

Rondeau
Provincial Park

Erieau

© Lucidmap Inc. 2015

Map 4-3: Rural Chatham-Kent

Map 4-3 Carte

Richardson Sdrd

Wheatley Rd

Carless Rd

Coatsworth Rd

Hornick Ln

Oak Rd

Quinn Ln

5

Ontario

Chat

Tilbury West And Romney Rd

1

Goodreau Ln

Herman Ln

6th Concession Ln

4

Kemp Ln

King & Whittle Rd

Cox Ln

5th Concession Ln

5th Concession Ln

Grove Rd

4th Concession Ln

Loose surface road
Route en gravier

4th Concession Ln

3rd Concession Ln

Loose s
Route en

WT

2nd Concession Ln

Coatsworth Rd

3rd Concession Ln

5

Campbell Rd

Stevenson Rd

Si

Zion Rd

Hodovick Rd

Wharram Rd

Ellerbeck Rd

Flat Rd

3

Talbot Tr

4

2nd Concession Ln

53

Lake Erie
Lac Érie

Scale

0   1   2 km

N

Great Lakes
Waterfront Trail

Le

2.0

H

Map 4-3: Rural Chatham-Kent

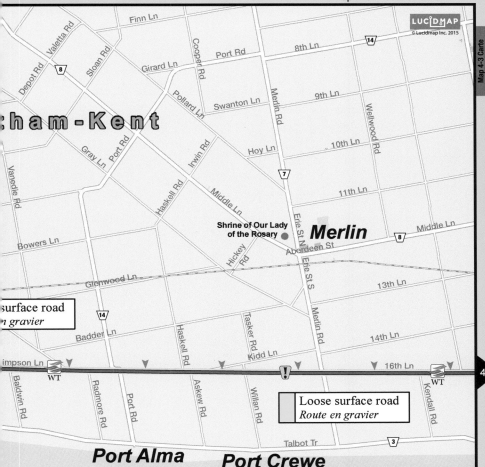

Map 4-3 Carte

LUCIDMAP
© Lucidmap Inc. 2015

:ham-Kent

Shrine of Our Lady
of the Rosary
Merlin
Aberdeen St

surface road
n gravier

Badder Ln

Loose surface road
Route en gravier

WT   WT   48

Port Alma   Port Crewe

Talbot Tr

Rural Chatham-Kent

---

egend / Légende

On-road / *Sur la route*	⊠ Campground / *Camping*	🍇 Winery / *Vinicole*
Off-road / *Hors route*	❓ Information / *Renseignements*	🌲 Conservation Area / *Zone de protection de la nature*
Alerts / *Alertes*	☀ Lookout / *Vue panoramique*	Provincial Park / *Parc provincial de l'Ontario*
.0▼ Distance / *Distance (km)*	⚓ Marina / *Marina*	Built-up / *Secteur bâti*
Connection / *Liaison*	℗ Parking / *Stationnement*	✝ Cemetery / *Cimetière*
Hospital / *Hôpital*	🏛 Town Hall / *Hôtel de ville*	Park, Natural Area / *Parc, Espace naturel*
Attraction / *Attraction*	🚻 Washrooms / *W.-C.*	Marsh / *Marais*
Beach / *Plage*		

51

Map 4-4: Wheatley / Point Pelee

Map 4-4 Carte

Great Lakes
Waterfront Trail

Legend / Légende

On-road / Sur la route
Off-road / Hors route
Alerts / Alertes
▼2.0▼ Distance / Distance (km)
Connection / Liaison
🏥 Hospital / Hôpital
● Attraction / Attraction
Beach / Plage
Campground / Camping
Information / Renseignements
Lookout / Vue panoramique
Marina / Marina

🍁 Carolinian Canada EcoTrail Site / Site du sentier écologique Carolinian Canada
Ⓟ Parking / Stationnement
🏛 Town Hall / Hôtel de ville
Washrooms / W.-C.
Winery / Vinicole
Conservation Area / Zone de protection de la nature
Provincial Park / Parc provincial de l'Ontario
Built-up / Secteur bâti
Cemetery / Cimetière
Park, Natural Area / Parc, Espace naturel
Marsh / Marais

Mersea Rd 11
Simpson Sdrd
Mersea Rd 10
Wheatley Rd

Two C
Conserva

1

Whea

Erie St N
Klonokye

Talbot Rd W
Middleton L

Erie St S
Pier Rd

W
Prov

77

Mersea Rd 4

Maneny Sdrd

34 **37** 🌳 **Kopegaron Woods Conservation Area**

33

Talbot Rd E

E s s e x

Milo Rd

!

Br
Po

Deer Run Rd

Fox Run Rd

Hillman Sdrd

WT

Oak St E   Mersea Rd 2

Deer Run Rd

● **Mennonite Home**

Danforth Av

S-turn / rough pavement. Narrow bridge / no shoulder
Virage en S. / pavé rugueux
Pont étroit / pas d'accotement

! Mersea Rd 2

37   🌅

L a k e
L a c

Seacliff Dr E   WT   Mersea Rd 1 ▼

Hillman Marsh Conservation Area

Erie Glen Manor   ●

20   Mersea Rd A   🌳

Bevel Line Rd

Mersea Rd B

Robson Rd

Beach Rd

Mersea Rd 19

Roundabout Exit onto Bevel Line Rd
Carrefour giratoire
Sortez sur Bevel Line Rd

! ⚓

🏕

N

33

Mersea Rd C

Scale
0   1   2 km

Point Pelee Dr

Mersea Rd D

Mersea Rd E

57

Map 4-4: Wheatley / Point Pelee

Chatham-Kent

Ontario

LUC**ID**MAP
© Lucidmap Inc. 2015

Map 4-4 Carte

Loose surface road
Route en gravier

WT

3

reeks
tion Area

Talbot Tr

atley

Rd

Wheatley
vincial Park

ridge (no shoulder)
nt (pas d'accotement)

e *Erie*
Érie

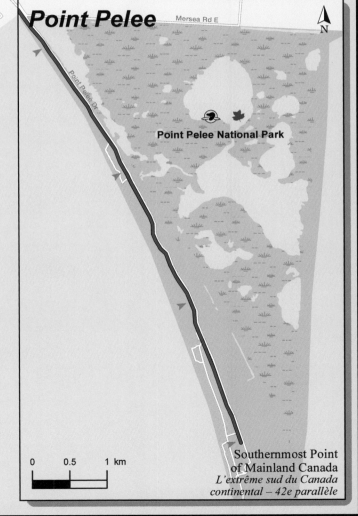

Point Pelee

Mersea Rd E

N

Point Pelee Dr

Point Pelee National Park

0   0.5   1 km

Southernmost Point
of Mainland Canada
*L'extrême sud du Canada
continental – 42e parallèle*

Wheatley / Point Pelee

Lakeshore

Tecumseh

Point Pelee National Park

Waterfront Trail : Section 5

Highlights of Section 5

Essex County has everything from the serenity of Pelee Island to the bustle of Windsor: award-winning wineries, celebrated culinary scene, fascinating museums, forts, beaches, farmstands, charming waterfront villages. Visit WaterfrontTrail.org, OntarioSouthwest.com and OntarioByBike.ca for additional tourism information and trip plans.

Trail Runs Along: Paved road shoulders, paved trails and screened limestone paths including the Chrysler Canada Greenway Rail Trail and the Ganatchio Trail in Windsor.
Essex County Waterfront Trail is part of the County-Wide Active Transportation Network (CWATS).
Length: 213.2 Kilometres

Kingsville / Leamington to Lakeshore Map Pages

Map 5-1: Kingsville / Leamington
Map 5-1B: Point Pelee
Map 5-2: Harrow / Colchester
Map 5-3: Amherstberg
Map 5-4: Windsor

Map 5-5: Windsor East
Map 5-6: Tecumseh
Map 5-7: Belle River
Map 5-8: Lakeshore

Map 5-1: Kingsville / Leamington

Kingsville

Woodland St

Sandybrook Way

Rd 2 E

N

29

Division Rd N

Fox La

Sumac Dr

Augustine Dr

Woodycrest Av

Jasperson la

Kratz Rd

3

Prince Albert St N

Division St N

Main St E

William Av

Remark Rd

Jasperson Dr

20

Seacliff Dr

WT

Mill St W

Main St W

McDonald St

Mill St W

Isadowne Av

Victoria Av

Trail

Lakeview Av

Main St W

James Av

Enter Chrysler Canada Greenway

Woodlawn Cr

Queen St

Division St S

Erie St

50

Park St

Dock Rd

Gate / Cyclist dismount
Barrière / Les cyclistes doivent descendre

Lawndale Av

Erie Av

Heritage Rd

Bush Dr

Lakeside Park

Ferry to Pelee Island

Narrow bridge /
No shoulder
*Pont étroit /
Pas d'accotement*

WT

0   0.5   1 km

Leamingt

Mor

Mersea Rd 3

Cameo D

Talbot St W

Leamington District Memorial H

34   48

Sandy Lake Dr

Maine Cr

Fraser Rd

Kenneth Dr

0   0.5   1 km

Rd 2 W

29

3rd Conc Rd

23

McCain Sdrd

Fox La

Kingsville

Main St W

Main St E

Cedar Creek Conservation Area

Chrysler Canada Greenway 42 kms

Main St W

Queen St

Wigle Av

20

Sea

Pleasant Valley Campground

Huffman Rd

Iler Rd

Arner Townline Rd

Cedar Creek Conservation Area

Lakeside Park

John R Park Homestead Conservation Area

Dolson Rd

Heritage Rd

50

WT

Cedar Island Park & Beach

Cedar Beach Conservation Area

P

Narrow bridge /
No shoulder
*Pont étroit /
Pas d'accotement*

Ferry to Pelee Island
Traversier à l'île Pelée

Clark Beach

Breezy Beach

Waters Beach

Little Essex Beach

Lake Erie
Lac Érie

L

Great Lakes
Waterfront Trail

Map 5-1: Kingsville / Leamington

Kingsville / Leamington

Scale

0   1   2 km

Legend / Légende

▬▬ On-road / Sur la route	⛺ Campground / Camping	🍇 Winery / Vinicole
▪ ▪ Off-road / Hors route	❓ Information / Renseignements	ⓖ Conservation Area / Zone de protection de la nature
❗ Alerts / Alertes	☀ Lookout / Vue panoramique	Provincial Park / Parc provincial de l'Ontario
2.0▼ Distance / Distance (km)	⚓ Marina / Marina	Built-up / Secteur bâti
▬▬ Connection / Liaison	Ⓟ Parking / Stationnement	✝✝ Cemetery / Cimetière
🅷 Hospital / Hôpital	🏛 Town Hall / Hôtel de ville	Park, Natural Area / Parc, Espace naturel
● Attraction / Attraction	🚻 Washrooms / W.-C.	Marsh / Marais
🏖 Beach / Plage		Trans Canada Trail / Sentier Transcanadien

Map 5-1B: Pelee Island

Map 5-1B Carte

Great Lakes
Waterfront Trail

Lake Erie
Lac Érie

E Shore Rd

Lorain Rd

LIGHTHOUSE POINT
PROVINCIAL NATURE RESERVE

Harris-Garno Rd

Clutton Rd

Brown's Rd

Parson's Rd

Scudder Rd

Dyke Rd

Ruggles Run

Centre Dyke Rd

N Shore Rd

Homeward Rd

Victoria Rd

W Pump Rd

Old Vineyard Rd

Pelee Airport

Rd

Ferry to Kingsville & Leamington
Traversier à Kingsville et Leamington

Visit
www.ontarioferries.com
or call **1-800-661-2220**
for schedules and other
information.

Visitez
www.ontarioferries.com
ou composez le 1-800-661-2220
pour obtenir les horaires et
autres renseignements.

N

Scale

0   0.5   1 km

Map 5-1B: Pelee Island

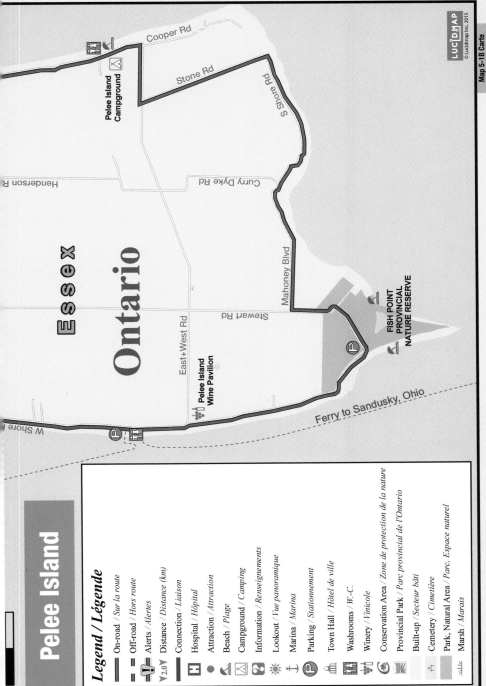

Map 5-1B Carte

© Lucidmap Inc. 2015

LUCIDMAP

59

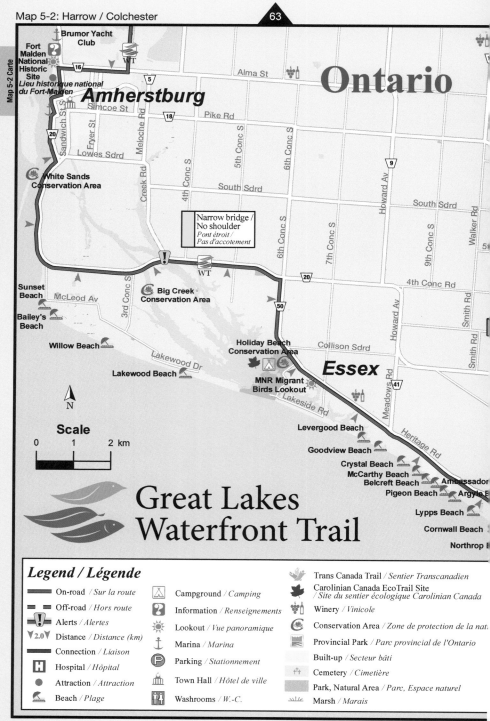

Map 5-2: Harrow / Colchester   63

Great Lakes Waterfront Trail

Legend / Légende

- On-road / Sur la route
- Off-road / Hors route
- ⚠ Alerts / Alertes
- ▼2.0▼ Distance / Distance (km)
- Connection / Liaison
- H Hospital / Hôpital
- ● Attraction / Attraction
- ⚓ Beach / Plage
- ⬠ Campground / Camping
- ❓ Information / Renseignements
- ☀ Lookout / Vue panoramique
- ⚓ Marina / Marina
- Ⓟ Parking / Stationnement
- 🏛 Town Hall / Hôtel de ville
- 🚻 Washrooms / W.-C.

- Trans Canada Trail / Sentier Transcanadien
- Carolinian Canada EcoTrail Site / Site du sentier écologique Carolinian Canada
- Winery / Vinicole
- Conservation Area / Zone de protection de la nat.
- Provincial Park / Parc provincial de l'Ontario
- Built-up / Secteur bâti
- Cemetery / Cimetière
- Park, Natural Area / Parc, Espace naturel
- Marsh / Marais

Map 5-2: Harrow / Colchester

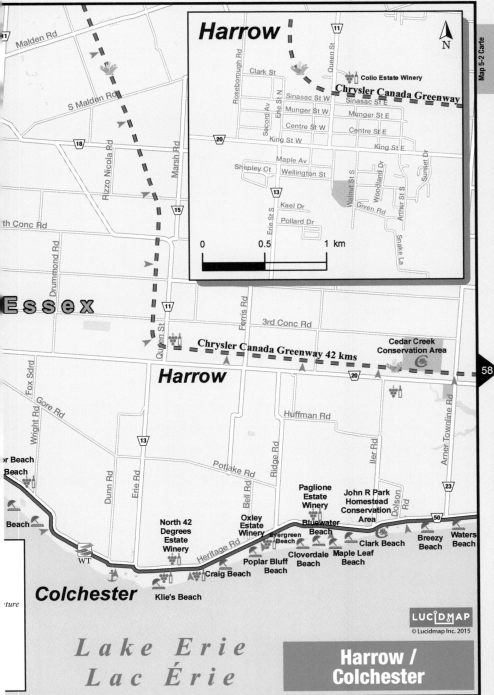

Harrow

N

Colio Estate Winery

Chrysler Canada Greenway

Roseborough Rd
Clark St
Sinasac St W
Sinasac St E
Munger St W
Munger St E
Centre St W
Centre St E
King St W
King St E
Maple Av
Shepley Ct
Wellington St
Kael Dr
Pollard Dr
Second Av
Erie St N
Queen St
Walnut St S
Woodland Dr
Arthur St S
Sunset Dr
Given Rd
Snake La
Erie St S

0   0.5   1 km

Essex

Chrysler Canada Greenway 42 kms

Cedar Creek
Conservation Area

Harrow

3rd Conc Rd
Ferris Rd
Huffman Rd
Potlake Rd
Ridge Rd
Bell Rd
Iler Rd
Dolson Rd
Arner Townline Rd
Queen St
Fox Sdrd
Wright Rd
Gore Rd
Dunn Rd
Erie Rd
Heritage Rd
Drummond Rd
Rizzo Nicola Rd
Marsh Rd
Malden Rd
S Malden Rd
th Conc Rd

58

23

50

r Beach
Beach

Beach

North 42
Degrees
Estate
Winery

Oxley
Estate
Winery

Paglione
Estate
Winery

John R Park
Homestead
Conservation
Area

Bluewater
Beach

Evergreen
Beach

Cloverdale
Beach

Clark Beach

Maple Leaf
Beach

Breezy
Beach

Waters
Beach

WT

Craig Beach

Poplar Bluff
Beach

Colchester   Klie's Beach

LUCIDMAP
© Lucidmap Inc. 2015

Lake Erie
Lac Érie

Harrow /
Colchester

61

Map 5-3: Amherstburg

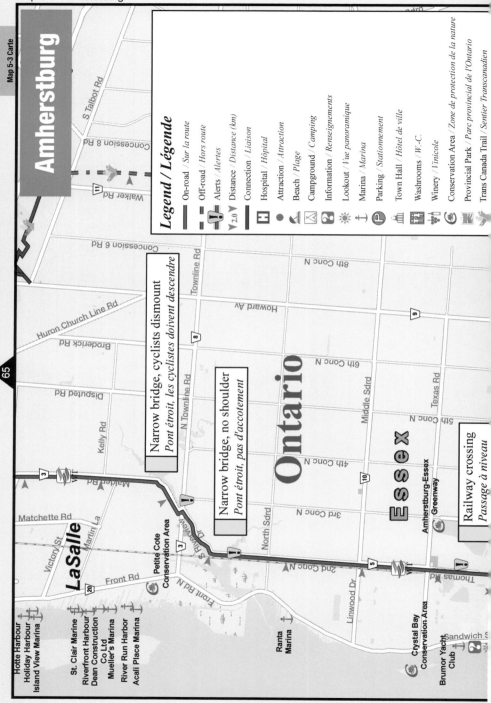

Amherstburg

Map 5-3 Carte

Legend / Légende

	On-road / Sur la route
	Off-road / Hors route
	Alerts / Alertes
	Distance / Distance (km)
	Connection / Liaison
	Hospital / Hôpital
	Attraction / Attraction
	Beach / Plage
	Campground / Camping
	Information / Renseignements
	Lookout / Vue panoramique
	Marina / Marina
	Parking / Stationnement
	Town Hall / Hôtel de ville
	Washrooms / W.-C.
	Winery / Vinicole
	Conservation Area / Zone de protection de la nature
	Provincial Park / Parc provincial de l'Ontario
	Trans Canada Trail / Sentier Transcanadien

Narrow bridge, cyclists dismount
Pont étroit, les cyclistes doivent descendre

Narrow bridge, no shoulder
Pont étroit, pas d'accotement

Railway crossing
Passage à niveau

Ontario

Essex

LaSalle

Hotte Harbour
Holiday Harbour
Island View Marina

St. Clair Marine
Riverfront Harbour
Dean Construction Co Ltd
Mueller's Marina
River Run Harbor
Acali Place Marina

Petite Cote Conservation Area

Ranta Marina

Crystal Bay Conservation Area

Brumor Yacht Club

Sandwich S

Amherstburg-Essex Greenway

S Talbot Rd
Concession 8 Rd
Walker Rd
Concession 6 Rd
Huron Church Line Rd
Broderick Rd
Disputed Rd
Kelly Rd
Malden Rd
Matchette Rd
Victory St
Martin La
Front Rd
N Townline Rd
Townline Rd
Howard Av
8th Conc N
6th Conc N
Middle Sdrd
Texas Rd
5th Conc N
4th Conc N
3rd Conc N
North Sdrd
S Riverview Rd
Front Rd N
Linwood Dr
2nd Conc N
Thomas Rd

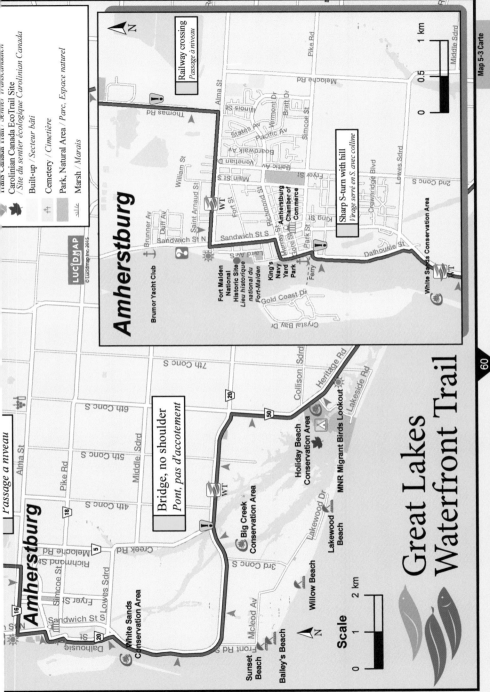

Map 5-3: Amherstburg

Amherstburg

Railway crossing
Passage à niveau

Trans Canada Trail / *Sentier Transcanadien*
Carolinian Canada EcoTrail Site
Site du sentier écologique Carolinian Canada
Built-up / *Secteur bâti*
Cemetery / *Cimetière*
Park, Natural Area / *Parc, Espace naturel*
Marsh / *Marais*

© Lucidmap Inc 2015.

N

1 km
0.5
0

Brumor Yacht Club

Fort Malden National Historic Site
Lieu historique national du Fort-Malden

King's Navy Yard Park

Amherstburg Chamber of Commerce

Sharp S-turn with hill
Virage serré en S, avec colline

White Sands Conservation Area

Gold Coast Dr
Crystal Bay Dr

Map 5-3 Carte

Amherstburg

Bridge, no shoulder
Pont, pas d'accotement

Big Creek Conservation Area

Holiday Beach Conservation Area

MNR Migrant Birds Lookout

Willow Beach

Sunset Beach

Bailey's Beach

White Sands Conservation Area

Scale

N

0   1   2 km

Great Lakes
Waterfront Trail

Passage à niveau

60

Map 5-4: Windsor

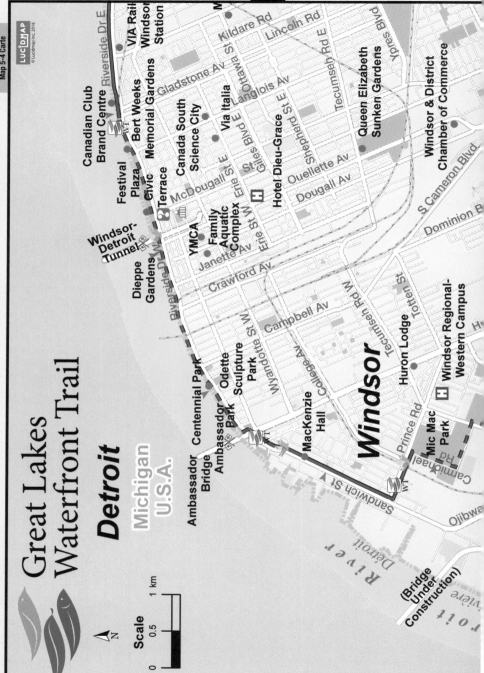

Great Lakes
Waterfront Trail

Detroit

Michigan
U.S.A.

Windsor

River Détroit

(Bridge Under Construction)

Scale

0   0.5   1 km

N

Map 5-4 Carte

LUC[D]MAP
© lucidmap inc 2016

Canadian Club
Brand Centre

VIA Rail
Windsor
Station

Riverside Dr E

Kildare Rd

Lincoln Rd

Festival
Plaza

Bert Weeks
Memorial Gardens

Gladstone Av

Ottawa St

Tecumseh Rd E

Ypres Blvd

Windsor
Civic
Terrace

Canada South
Science City

Via Italia

Langlois Av

Queen Elizabeth
Sunken Gardens

Windsor-
Detroit
Tunnel

Dieppe
Gardens

McDougall St

Giles Blvd E

Erie St E

Shepherd St E

Hotel Dieu-Grace

Ouellette Av

Windsor & District
Chamber of Commerce

YMCA

Family
Aquatic
Complex

Erie St W

Dougall Av

S. Cameron Blvd

Janette Av

Dominion B

Riverside Dr W

Crawford Av

Campbell Av

Tecumseh Rd W

Huron Lodge

Totten St

Windsor Regional-
Western Campus

H

Ambassador
Bridge

Centennial Park

Odette
Sculpture
Park

Ambassador
Park

Wyandotte St W

College Av

MacKenzie
Hall

Prince Rd

Mic Mac
Park

Camichael Rd

Sandwich St W

Ojibwa

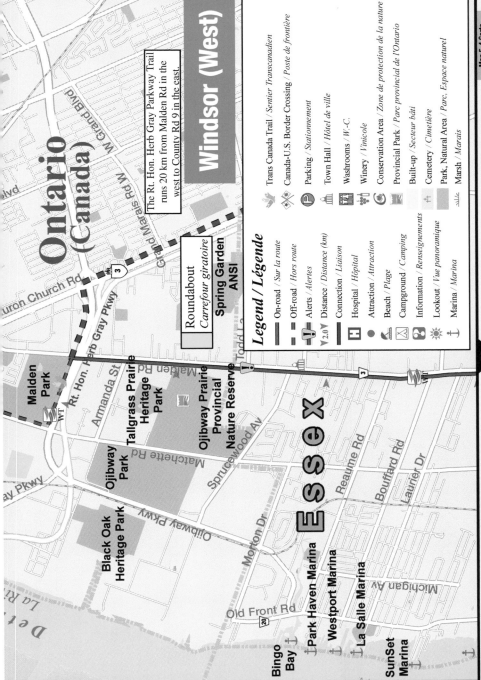

Map 5-4: Windsor

Map 5-4 Carte

Windsor (West)

The Rt. Hon. Herb Gray Parkway Trail runs 20 km from Malden Rd in the west to County Rd 9 in the east.

Legend / Légende

Roundabout / *Carrefour giratoire*

Spring Garden ANSI

On-road / *Sur la route*	
Off-road / *Hors route*	
Alerts / *Alertes*	
▼2.0▼ Distance / *Distance (km)*	
Connection / *Liaison*	
H Hospital / *Hôpital*	
● Attraction / *Attraction*	
Beach / *Plage*	
Campground / *Camping*	
Information / *Renseignements*	
☀ Lookout / *Vue panoramique*	
Marina / *Marina*	

Trans Canada Trail / *Sentier Transcanadien*	
Canada-U.S. Border Crossing / *Poste de frontière*	
P Parking / *Stationnement*	
Town Hall / *Hôtel de ville*	
Washrooms / *W.-C.*	
Winery / *Vinicole*	
Conservation Area / *Zone de protection de la nature*	
Provincial Park / *Parc provincial de l'Ontario*	
Built-up / *Secteur bâti*	
† Cemetery / *Cimetière*	
Park, Natural Area / *Parc. Espace naturel*	
Marsh / *Marais*	

Ontario (Canada)

W Grand Marais Rd W

Grand Marais Rd W

Huron Church Rd

3

Malden Rd

Todd Ln

W. Rt. Hon. Herb Gray Pkwy

Rt. Hon. Herb Gray Pkwy

Malden Park

Armanda St

Amanda St

Tallgrass Prairie Heritage Park

Ojibway Prairie Provincial Nature Reserve

Matchette Rd

Ojibway Park

Sprucewood Av

Black Oak Heritage Park

Ojibway Pkwy

...ay Pkwy

Essex

Morton Dr

Reaume Rd

Bouffard Rd

Laurier Dr

Michigan Av

Old Front Rd

20

Bingo Bay ⚓

Park Haven Marina ⚓

Westport Marina ⚓

La Salle Marina ⚓

SunSet Marina

De...
La Ri...

62

65

Map 5-5: Windsor East

Map 5-5 Carte

Great Lakes
Waterfront Trail

Lake St. Clair
Lac Sainte-Claire

Sandpoint Beach

Lakeview Marina

Riverside Dr E

WT

Little River Blvd

McHugh St

Tecumseh Rd

Forest Glade Dr

Riverdale Av

Little River Rd

Lauzon Rd

Lauzon Pkwy

WT

Wyandotte St E

Jefferson Blvd

Windsor

S National St

Coventry Gardens

Pillette Rd

Reaume Park

Seminole St

Central Av

mouth Rd

Chrys

Scale

N

0   0.5   1 km

Market Square

Drouillard Rd

Walker Rd

Kildare Rd

WT

H Windsor Regional -
Metropolitan Campus

Blvd

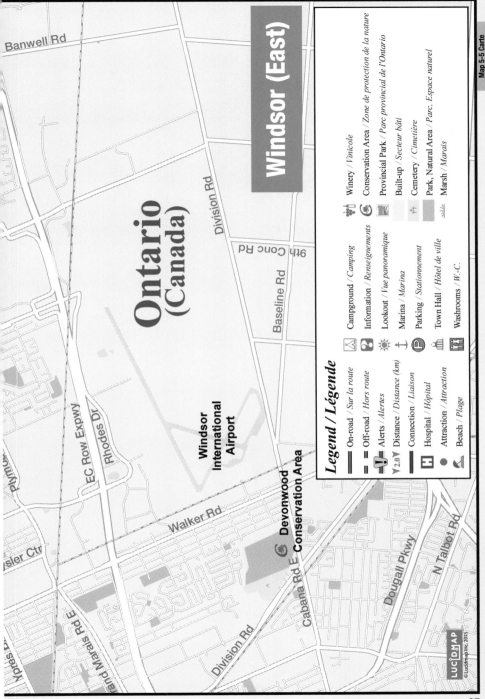

Map 5-5: Windsor East

Map 5-5 Carte

Windsor (East)

Ontario
(Canada)

Banwell Rd

Division Rd

9th Conc Rd

Baseline Rd

Windsor
International
Airport

EC Row Expwy

Rhodes Dr

Walker Rd

Devonwood
Conservation Area

Cabana Rd E

Dougall Pkwy

N Talbot Rd

Division Rd

Grand Marais Rd E

Ypres Bl...

Chrysler Ctr

Legend / Légende

On-road / Sur la route	
Off-road / Hors route	
Alerts / Alertes	
▼2.0▼ Distance / Distance (km)	
Connection / Liaison	
H Hospital / Hôpital	
● Attraction / Attraction	
Beach / Plage	

Campground / Camping	
Information / Renseignements	
Lookout / Vue panoramique	
Marina / Marina	
P Parking / Stationnement	
Town Hall / Hôtel de ville	
Washrooms / W.-C.	

Winery / Vinicole	
Conservation Area / Zone de protection de la nature	
Provincial Park / Parc provincial de l'Ontario	
Built-up / Secteur bâti	
Cemetery / Cimetière	
Park, Natural Area / Parc, Espace naturel	
Marsh / Marais	

Map 5-6: Tecumseh

Map 5-6 Carte

Great Lakes
Waterfront Trail

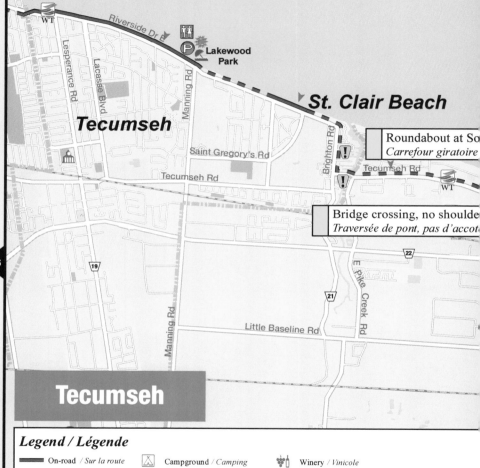

Riverside Dr E

WT

Lakewood
Park

Lesperance Rd

Lacasse Blvd

Manning Rd

St. Clair Beach

Tecumseh

Saint Gregory's Rd

Brighton Rd

Roundabout at So
Carrefour giratoire

Tecumseh Rd

WT

Tecumseh Rd

Bridge crossing, no shoulde
Traversée de pont, pas d'accot

66

19

22

E Pike Creek Rd

21

Manning Rd

Little Baseline Rd

Tecumseh

Legend / Légende

▬▬▬ On-road / *Sur la route*	🏕 Campground / *Camping*	🍷 Winery / *Vinicole*
▬ ▬ Off-road / *Hors route*	ℹ Information / *Renseignements*	Ⓒ Conservation Area / *Zone de protection de la nature*
⚠ Alerts / *Alertes*	☀ Lookout / *Vue panoramique*	Provincial Park / *Parc provincial de l'Ontario*
▼2.0▼ Distance / *Distance (km)*	⚓ Marina / *Marina*	Built-up / *Secteur bâti*
Connection / *Liaison*	Ⓟ Parking / *Stationnement*	✝ Cemetery / *Cimetière*
🏥 Hospital / *Hôpital*	🏛 Town Hall / *Hôtel de ville*	Park, Natural Area / *Parc. Espace naturel*
● Attraction / *Attraction*	🚻 Washrooms / *W.-C.*	Marsh / *Marais*
Beach / *Plage*		

Map 5-6: Tecumseh

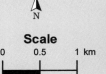

Map 5-6 Carte

Lake St. Clair
Lac Sainte-Claire

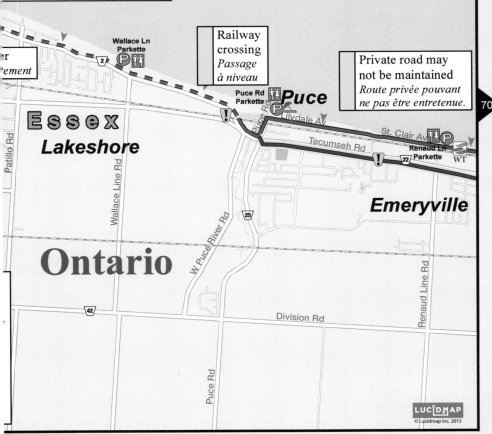

...uthwind Cres. and at Aloha Dr.
...à Southwind Cres. et à Aloha Dr.

Wallace Ln
Parkette

Railway
crossing
*Passage
à niveau*

Private road may
not be maintained
*Route privée pouvant
ne pas être entretenue.*

70

Puce Rd
Parkette

Puce

Lilydale Av

St. Clair Av

Tecumseh Rd

Renaud Ln
Parkette

WT

Essex

Lakeshore

Patillo Rd

Wallace Line Rd

Emeryville

W Puce River Rd

Ontario

Renaud Line Rd

Division Rd

Puce Rd

LUCIDMAP
© Lucidmap Inc. 2015

Map 5-7: Belle River

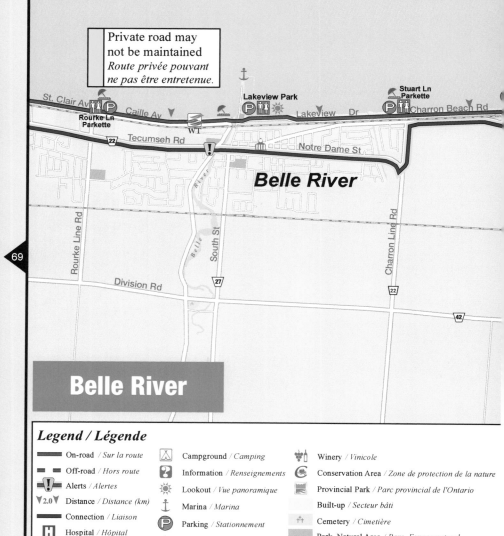

Map 5-7 Carte

Great Lakes
Waterfront Trail

L a k
L a c   S

**Private road may
not be maintained**
*Route privée pouvant
ne pas être entretenue.*

St. Clair Av

Lakeview Park

**Stuart Ln
Parkette**

Caille Av

Lakeview   Dr

Charron Beach Rd

**Rourke Ln
Parkette**

WT

22   Tecumseh Rd

Notre Dame St

Belle River

Rourke Line Rd

Belle

South St

27

Division Rd

Charron Line Rd

22

42

Belle River

Legend / Légende

▬▬	On-road / *Sur la route*	⊠	Campground / *Camping*	🍇	Winery / *Vinicole*
▬ ▬	Off-road / *Hors route*	❓	Information / *Renseignements*	🍃	Conservation Area / *Zone de protection de la nature*
❗	Alerts / *Alertes*	☀	Lookout / *Vue panoramique*		Provincial Park / *Parc provincial de l'Ontario*
▼2.0▼	Distance / *Distance (km)*	⚓	Marina / *Marina*		Built-up / *Secteur bâti*
▬	Connection / *Liaison*	Ⓟ	Parking / *Stationnement*	✝✝	Cemetery / *Cimetière*
H	Hospital / *Hôpital*	🏛	Town Hall / *Hôtel de ville*		Park, Natural Area / *Parc, Espace naturel*
●	Attraction / *Attraction*	🚻	Washrooms / *W.-C.*	〜	Marsh / *Marais*
🏖	Beach / *Plage*				

69

Map 5-7: Belle River

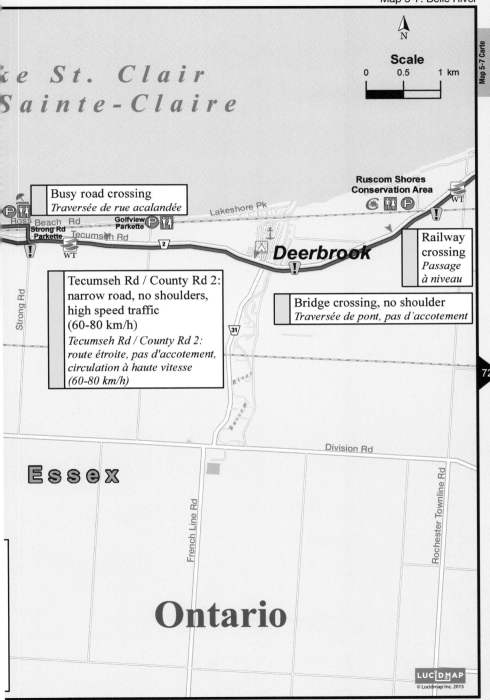

Scale

0   0.5   1 km

N

Map 5-7 Carte

ke St. Clair
Sainte-Claire

Ruscom Shores
Conservation Area

WT

Busy road crossing
Traversée de rue acalandée

Lakeshore Pk

Ross Beach Rd
Strong Rd
Parkette   Tecumseh Rd

Golfview
Parkette

2

Deerbrook

Railway
crossing
*Passage
à niveau*

WT

Tecumseh Rd / County Rd 2:
narrow road, no shoulders,
high speed traffic
(60-80 km/h)
Tecumseh Rd / County Rd 2:
route étroite, pas d'accotement,
circulation à haute vitesse
(60-80 km/h)

Bridge crossing, no shoulder
Traversée de pont, pas d'accotement

Strong Rd

31

River

Ruscom

72

Division Rd

Essex

Rochester Townline Rd

French Line Rd

Ontario

LUCIDMAP
© Lucidmap Inc. 2015

Map 5-8: Lakeshore

Great Lakes Waterfront Trail

Map 5-8 Carte

L a

L a c

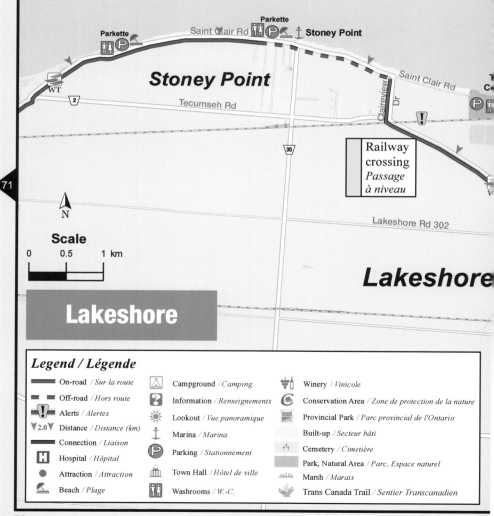

Parkette

Saint Clair Rd · Stoney Point

Parkette

Stoney Point

WT

2

Tecumseh Rd

Saint Clair Rd

Clairview Dr

35

Railway crossing
Passage à niveau

Lakeshore Rd 302

N

Scale

0   0.5   1 km

Lakeshore

Legend / Légende

—— On-road / *Sur la route*	🏕 Campground / *Camping*
– – Off-road / *Hors route*	❗ Information / *Renseignements*
❗ Alerts / *Alertes*	☀ Lookout / *Vue panoramique*
▼2.0▼ Distance / *Distance (km)*	⚓ Marina / *Marina*
—— Connection / *Liaison*	Ⓟ Parking / *Stationnement*
🄷 Hospital / *Hôpital*	🏛 Town Hall / *Hôtel de ville*
● Attraction / *Attraction*	🚻 Washrooms / *W.-C.*
🏖 Beach / *Plage*	

🍷 Winery / *Vinicole*	
🌿 Conservation Area / *Zone de protection de la nature*	
Provincial Park / *Parc provincial de l'Ontario*	
Built-up / *Secteur bâti*	
✝✝ Cemetery / *Cimetière*	
Park, Natural Area / *Parc, Espace naturel*	
Marsh / *Marais*	
🍁 Trans Canada Trail / *Sentier Transcanadien*	

71

Map 5-8: Lakeshore

Map 5-8 Carte

Lake St. Clair
Lac Sainte-Claire

Lighthouse
Conservation Area

Lighthouse Cove

Lighthouse
Inn

Thames
River

Tremblay Beach
Conservation Area

Laforet Beach Rd

Couture Beach Rd

Gracey Sdrd
Parkette

Lakeshore Rd 301

Tisdelle Dr

Gracey Sdrd

E s s e x

Lighthouse Rd

Tecumseh Rd

WT

Railway
crossing
Passage
à niveau

77

Tecumseh Rd

2

37

39

WT

2

Tecumseh Rd / County Rd 2: narrow road, no shoulders, high speed traffic (80 km/h)
Tecumseh Rd / County Rd 2: route étroite, pas d'accotement, circulation à haute vitesse (80 km/h)

Lakeshore Rd 303

Ontario

42

Division Rd

401

LUCIDMAP
© Lucidmap Inc. 2015

30km to Leamington

Grand Bend, Lambton Shores

Photo: Tourism Sarnia-Lambton

Sarnia

Photo: Tourism Sarnia-Lambton

Waterfront Trail : Section 6

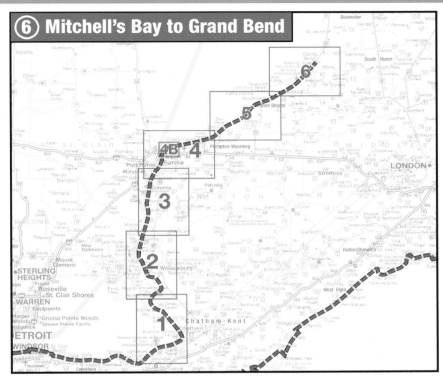

(6) Mitchell's Bay to Grand Bend

Highlights of Section 6
Traveling along the St. Clair River and Lake Huron in Ontario's Blue Water Country, stunning beaches, ferries to Michigan, art galleries, theatre and craft breweries, world's best food truck fries in Point Edward, the Pinery Provincial Park and Grand Bend - a vibrant beach community.

Trail Runs Along: Rural roads with some gravel sections, roads with paved shoulders and paved trails. This section of the Waterfront Trail is part of St. Clair River Trail and the Bluewater Trails.
Length: 208 Kilometres

Mitchell's Bay to Grand Bend Map Pages
Map 6-1: Mitchell's Bay
Map 6-2: Wallaceburg
Map 6-3: St. Clair Township
Map 6-4: Sarnia
Map 6-4B: Sarnia / Port Edward
Map 6-5: Lambton Shores
Map 6-6: Grand Bend

Map 6-1: Mitchell's Bay

Map 6-1 Carte

Mitchell's Bay

Ontario

Union Ln

Saint Clair Rd

[40]

Cedar Hedge Ln

Countryview Ln

[29]

Claymore Ln

[43]

Belle Rose Ln

[37]

Baldoon Rd

Greenvalley Ln

Bush Ln

Rivard Ln

Electric Ln

[42]

Bear Line Rd

[43]

[42]

Kennedy Rd

Mallard Ln

[34]

William Lewis Ln

Mud Creek Ln

Bay Ln

Mitchell's Bay

Winter Line Rd

Saint Philippes Ln

Marsh Ln

Angler Ln

Big Pointe Rd

Main St

South Lakeshore Trail

Gravel road
Route en gravier

[P]

79

Legend / Légende

On-road / *Sur la route*	
Off-road / *Hors route*	
Alerts / *Alertes*	
▼2.0 Distance / *Distance (km)*	
Connection / *Liaison*	
H Hospital / *Hôpital*	
● Attraction / *Attraction*	
Beach / *Plage*	
Campground / *Camping*	
Information / *Renseignements*	
☀ Lookout / *Vue panoramique*	
⚓ Marina / *Marina*	
P Parking / *Stationnement*	
Town Hall / *Hôtel de ville*	
Washrooms / *W.-C.*	
Winery / *Vinicole*	
Conservation Area / *Zone de protection de la nature*	
Provincial Park / *Parc provincial de l'Ontario*	
Trans Canada Trail / *Sentier Transcanadien*	
Built-up / *Secteur bâti*	
Cemetery / *Cimetière*	
Park, Natural Area / *Parc, Espace naturel*	
Marsh / *Marais*	

N

Scale

© Lucidmap Inc. 2015

Map 6-1: Mitchell's Bay

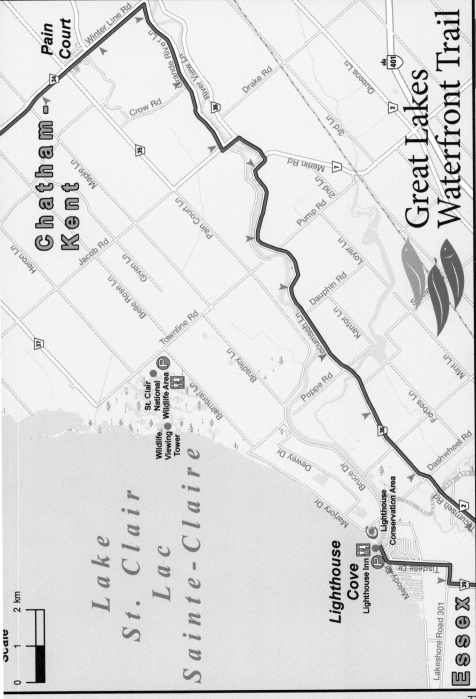

Great Lakes
Waterfront Trail

Map 6-1 Carte

73

77

Map 6-2: Wallaceburg

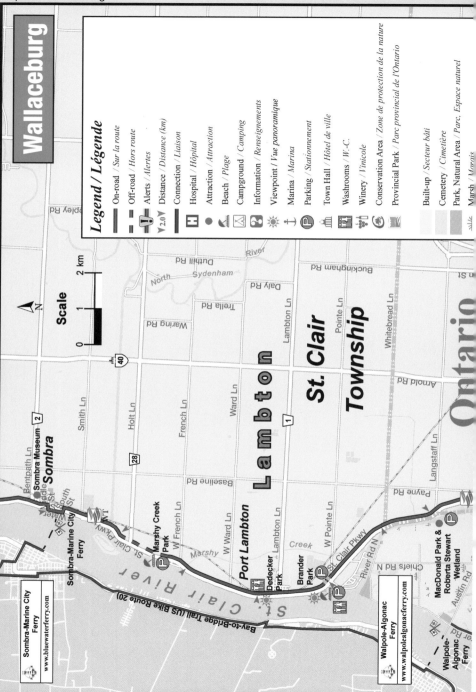

Map 6-2 Carte

Wallaceburg

Map 6-2: Wallaceburg

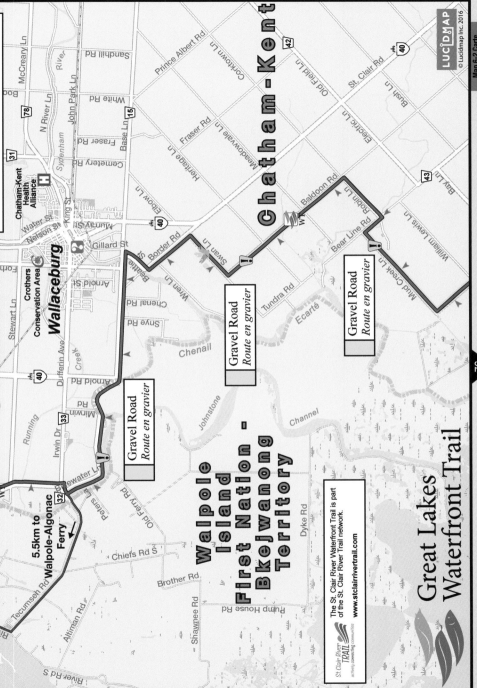

Chatham-Kent

Wallaceburg

Chatham-Kent Health Alliance

Crothers Conservation Area

Walpole Island First Nation - Bkejwanong Territory

Gravel Road
Route en gravier

Gravel Road
Route en gravier

Gravel Road
Route en gravier

5.5km to Walpole-Algonac Ferry

The St. Clair River Waterfront Trail is part of the St. Clair River Trail network.

www.stclairrivertrail.com

St Clair River TRAIL
actively connecting communities

Great Lakes Waterfront Trail

© Lucidmap Inc. 2016

Map 6-2 Carte

76

79

Map 6-3: St. Clair Townshiip

Map 6-3 Carte

Great Lakes
Waterfront Trail

Ontario

Lambton

The St. Clair River Waterfront Trail is part of the St. Clair River Trail network.

St. Clair River TRAIL
actively connecting communities

www.stclairrivertrail.com

Telfer Rd

Plank Rd

20

4

Waubuno Rd

31

Kimball Rd

31

Indian Rd S

Tecumseh Rd

Scott Rd

Ladysmith Rd

Petrolia Ln

Rokeby Ln

Moore Ln

Degurse Dr

40

Tashmoo Ave

40

Lasalle Ln

4

Vidal St

35

St. Clair Pkwy

Guthrie Park

Beckwith St

Veterans Way

Cameron St

Lyndoch St

Corunna

Mooretown Campground

Mooretown Sports Complex

Moore Museum

Mooretown

Mooretown Centennial Park

Clair Pkwy

St. Clair River

Bay-to-Bridge Trail

(US Bike Route 20)

N

Scale

0   1   2 km

80

Map 6-3: St. Clair Township

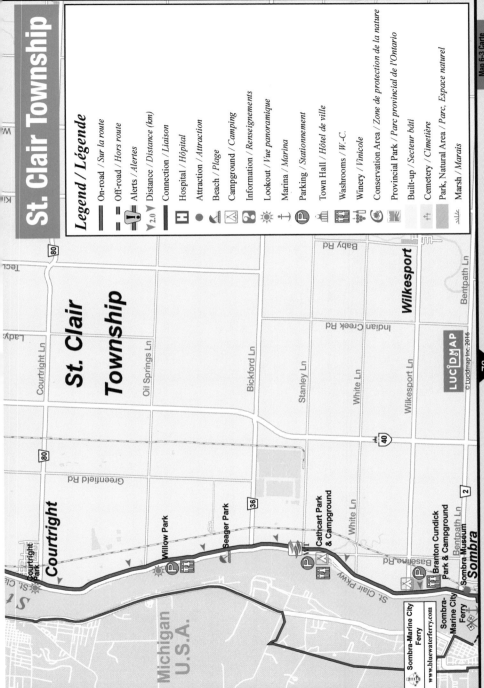

St. Clair Township

Legend / Légende

- On-road / Sur la route
- Off-road / Hors route
- Alerts / Alertes
- 2.0 Distance / Distance (km)
- Connection / Liaison
- Hospital / Hôpital
- Attraction / Attraction
- Beach / Plage
- Campground / Camping
- Information / Renseignements
- Lookout / Vue panoramique
- Marina / Marina
- Parking / Stationnement
- Town Hall / Hôtel de ville
- Washrooms / W.-C.
- Winery / Vinicole
- Conservation Area / Zone de protection de la nature
- Provincial Park / Parc provincial de l'Ontario
- Built-up / Secteur bâti
- Cemetery / Cimetière
- Park, Natural Area / Parc, Espace naturel
- Marsh / Marais

St. Clair Township

Courtright

Wilkesport

Sombra

Courtright Ln
Oil Springs Ln
Bickford Ln
Stanley Ln
White Ln
Wilkesport Ln
Bentpath Ln
Baby Rd
Indian Creek Rd

Greenfield Rd
Courtright Park
Willow Park
Seager Park
Cathcart Park & Campground
St. Clair Pkwy
Baseline Rd
Branton Cundick Park & Campground
Sombra Museum
Bentpath Ln

Michigan U.S.A.

Sombra-Marine City Ferry
www.bluewaterferry.com

Sombra-Marine City Ferry

Sombra-Marine City Ferry

LUCIDMAP
© Lucidmap Inc. 2016

78

81

Map 6-4: Sarnia

Map 6-4 Carte

Great Lakes
Waterfront Trail

Lake
Lac

Bridge To Bay Trail

Bluewater Bridge
No pedestrians. No cyclists.
Aucun piéton. Aucun cycliste.
www.bluewaterbridge.ca

Baxter Park

WT

Lakeshore Rd

7

Canatara Park

Cathcart Blvd

Howard Wa
Natural path
cyclists and

27

Lighthouse

Waterfront Park

19

Sarnia

Michigan Ave

Point Edward
Community Centre

Bluewater
Bridge

Casino

Venetian Blvd

29

Indian Rd N

Murphy Rd

Blackwell Rd

Wawanosh Wetlands
Conservation Area

402

Bridgeview Marina

Guthrie Dr W.

Exmouth St

Howard Watson Nature Trail

Great Lakes Monument
Sarnia Bay Marina

Centennial
Park

Maxwell St

16

Findl Dr

Modeland Rd

*Port
Huron*

Heritage Downtown

Bluewater
Health

H

London Rd

Front St

Rainbow
Park

Campbell St

25

Confederation St

*Michigan
U.S.A.*

St. Clair River

Christina St S

Vidal St S

Andrew
St

Imperial Ave

Indian Rd S

McGregor Sdrd

40

L

(US Bike Route 20)

34

Churchill Ln

Tashmoo Ave

Degurse Dr

Scott Rd

Indian Rd S

Kimball Rd

Plank Rd

14

31

Bridge To Bay Trail

St. Clair Pkwy

WT

Vidal St

40

Aamjiwnaang First Nation
(former Chippewas of Sarnia)

35

Lasalle

Line

McGregor Sdrd

D

LUCiDMAP
© Lucidmap Inc. 2015

Map 6-4: Sarnia

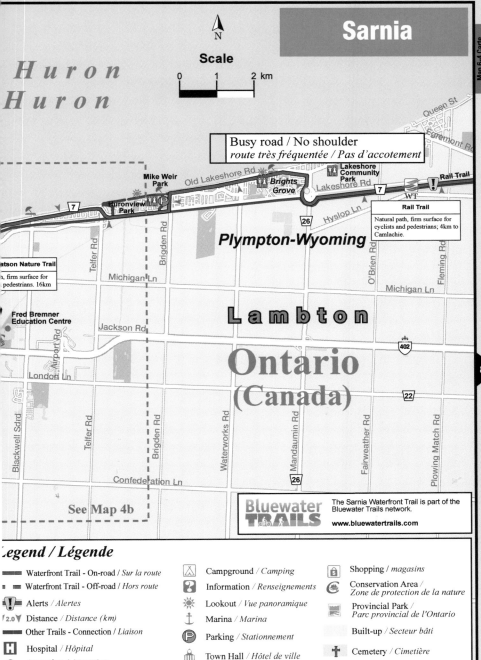

Sarnia

Map 6-4 Carte

Huron
Huron

Scale

0   1   2 km

Busy road / No shoulder
route très fréquentée / Pas d'accotement

Queen St

Egremont Rd

Mike Weir Park

Old Lakeshore Rd

Lakeshore Community Park

Rail Trail

Brights Grove

Lakeshore Rd

Euronview Park

7

WT

Rail Trail

Natural path, firm surface for cyclists and pedestrians; 4km to Camlachie.

7

26

Hyslop Ln

Plympton-Wyoming

O'Brien Rd

Fleming Rd

atson Nature Trail

..., firm surface for
pedestrians. 16km

Telfer Rd

Michigan Ln

Brigden Rd

Michigan Ln

**Fred Bremner
Education Centre**

Jackson Rd

Lambton

Airport Rd

402

84

Ontario
(Canada)

London Ln

Blackwell Sdrd

Telfer Rd

Brigden Rd

Waterworks Rd

Mandaumin Rd

Fairweather Rd

Plowing Match Rd

22

26

See Map 4b

Confederation Ln

**Bluewater
TRAILS**

The Sarnia Waterfront Trail is part of the
Bluewater Trails network.

www.bluewatertrails.com

Legend / Légende

- ▬▬ Waterfront Trail - On-road / *Sur la route*
- ▪ ▪ Waterfront Trail - Off-road / *Hors route*
- ⚠ Alerts / *Alertes*
- ▾2.0▾ Distance / *Distance (km)*
- ▬▬ Other Trails - Connection / *Liaison*
- Ⓗ Hospital / *Hôpital*
- ● Attraction / *Attraction*
- ⚓ Beach / *Plage*

- ◭ Campground / *Camping*
- ❓ Information / *Renseignements*
- ☀ Lookout / *Vue panoramique*
- ⚓ Marina / *Marina*
- Ⓟ Parking / *Stationnement*
- 🏛 Town Hall / *Hôtel de ville*
- 🚻 Washrooms / *W.-C.*

- 🛍 Shopping / *magasins*
- Ⓒ Conservation Area / *Zone de protection de la nature*
- Provincial Park / *Parc provincial de l'Ontario*
- Built-up / *Secteur bâti*
- ✝ Cemetery / *Cimetière*
- Park, Natural Area / *Parc, Espace naturel*

Map 6-4B: Sarnia / Point Edward Detail Map

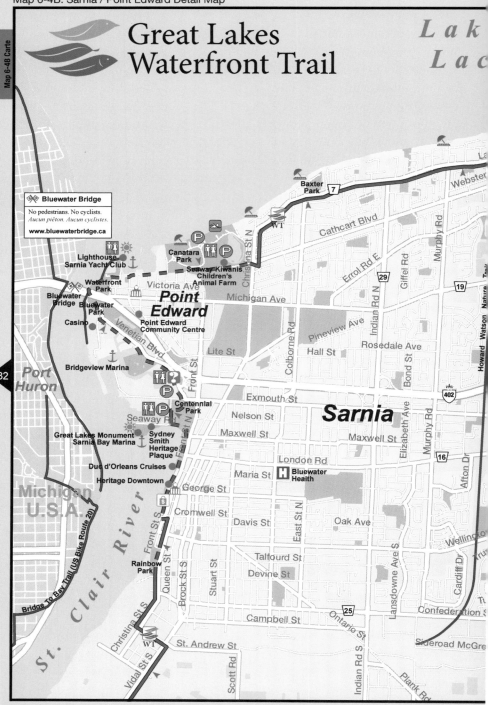

Great Lakes
Waterfront Trail

L a k
L a c

Map 6-4B Carte

Bluewater Bridge

No pedestrians. No cyclists.
Aucun piéton. Aucun cyclistes.

www.bluewaterbridge.ca

Baxter
Park   7

Webster

Cathcart Blvd

WT

Lighthouse
Sarnia Yacht Club

Canatara
Park

Seaway Kiwanis
Children's
Animal Farm

Errol Rd E

29

Giffel Rd

Murphy Rd

19

Waterfront
Park

Victoria Ave

**Point
Edward**

Michigan Ave

Indian Rd N

Nature Trail

Bluewater
Bridge

Bluewater
Park

Casino

Point Edward
Community Centre

Venetian Blvd

Colborne Rd

Pineview Ave

Rosedale Ave

Howard Watson

Lite St

Hall St

Bond St

402

Bridgeview Marina

Front St

82   **Port
Huron**

Centennial
Park

Exmouth St

Sarnia

Murphy Rd

Nelson St

Elizabeth Ave

16

Seaway Rd

Great Lakes Monument
Sarnia Bay Marina

Maxwell St

Maxwell St

Afton Dr

Sydney
Smith
Heritage
Plaque

London Rd

Duc d'Orleans Cruises

Maria St   **H** Bluewater
Health

Heritage Downtown

George St

**Michigan
U.S.A.**

Cromwell St

Davis St

East St N

Oak Ave

Wellington

Front St S

Cardiff Dr

Front St S

Talfourd St

Lansdowne Ave S

Rainbow
Park

Queen St

Stuart St

Devine St

Brock St S

St. Clair River

Confederation S

25

Bridge To Bay Trail (US Bike Route 20)

Christina St S

Campbell St

Ontario St

Sideroad McGre

Vidal St S

WT

St. Andrew St

Scott Rd

Indian Rd S

Plank Rd

Map 6-4B: Sarnia / Point Edward Detail Map

Sarnia /
Point Edward

Huronview
Park

Map 6-4B Carte

Lakeshore Rd

Clarence St WT

7

e Huron

Huron

keshore Rd

Dr

Howard Watson Nature Trail

Natural path, firm surface for
cyclists and pedestrians. 16 km

Lambton

Michigan Ln

Blackwell Rd

Wheatley Dr

Telfer Rd

Ontario
(Canada)

The Rapids Pkwy

27

Fred Bremner
Education Centre

Wawanosh Wetlands
Conservation Area

Ube Dr

Jackson Rd

Airport Rd

402

83

Quinn Dr

Blackwell Sdrd

London Ln

22

Finch Dr

40

Bluewater TRAILS The Sarnia Waterfront Trail is part of the
Bluewater Trails network.

www.bluewatertrails.com

n St

deau Dr

Modeland Rd

Upper Canada Dr

rner Dr

St

egor

Legend / Légende

— Waterfront Trail - On-road / *Sur la route*

▬ ▬ Waterfront Trail - Off-road / *Hors route*

⚠ Alerts / *Alertes*

▼2.0▼ Distance / *Distance (km)*

— Other Trails - Connection / *Liaison*

H Hospital / *Hôpital*

● Attraction / *Attraction*

⚓ Beach / *Plage*

⛺ Campground / *Camping*

❓ Information / *Renseignements*

☀ Lookout / *Vue panoramique*

⚓ Marina / *Marina*

Ⓟ Parking / *Stationnement*

🏛 Town Hall / *Hôtel de ville*

🚻 Washrooms / *W.-C.*

Conservation Area /
Zone de protection de la nature

Provincial Park /
Parc provincial de l'Ontario

Built-up / *Secteur bâti*

✝ Cemetery / *Cimetière*

Park, Natural Area /
Parc, Espace naturel

LUCIDMAP
© Lucidmap Inc. 2015

85

Map 6-5: Lambton Shores

Great Lakes
Waterfront Trail

Map 6-5 Carte

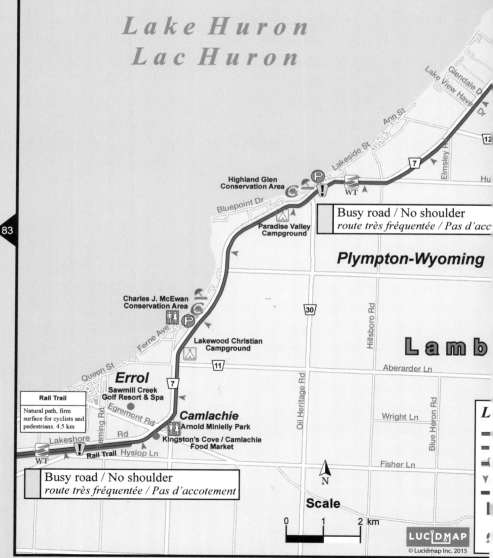

Lake Huron
Lac Huron

Glendale D

Lake View Haven Dr

Ann St

Lakeside St

12

7

Elmsley R

Hu

Highland Glen
Conservation Area

P

WT

Bluepoint Dr

Busy road / No shoulder
route très fréquentée / Pas d'acc

Paradise Valley
Campground

83

Plympton-Wyoming

Charles J. McEwan
Conservation Area

30

Hillsboro Rd

L a m b

P

Lakewood Christian
Campground

Ferne Ave

Aberarder Ln

11

Queen St

Errol

7

Oil Heritage Rd

Wright Ln

Blue Heron Rd

Sawmill Creek
Golf Resort & Spa

Rail Trail
Natural path, firm surface for cyclists and pedestrians. 4.5 km

Fleming Rd

Egremont Rd

Camlachie

Arnold Minielly Park

Kingston's Cove / Camlachie
Food Market

Fisher Ln

Lakeshore

Rd

Hyslop Ln

Rail Trail

WT

Busy road / No shoulder
route très fréquentée / Pas d'accotement

N

Scale

0   1   2 km

LUC[D]MAP

© Lucidmap Inc. 2015

L

Kettle and
Stony Point
First Nation

Indian La

Wood Dr

berwash

Indian Hills
Golf Course

WT

21

7

Cliff Rd

Oak Ave

Lakeshore Rd

Trail W

Indian Hills
Trail W

Lambton Shores

Thomson Ln

Kinnaird Rd

6

Lambton Shores
3

Ridge Rd

Proof Ln

Fuller Rd

Rawlings Rd

Jericho Rd

Ontario

Cedar Point Ln

Dolmage Rd

2

ubbard Ln

Townsend Ln

cotement

Main St

King St

Rawlings Rd

Amy Camp Rd

Jura Ln

Forest

12

Esli Dodge
Conservation
Area

Douglas Ln

Hickory Creek Ln

Uttoxeter Rd

Brush Rd

Forest Rd

21

Elarton Rd

1st School Rd

Bethel Rd

ton

Aberarder Vineyard /
Bed & Breakfast

11

Birnam Ln

Rd

Legend / Légende

▬▬▬ Waterfront Trail - On-road / Sur la route	🏕 Campground / Camping	🛍 Shopping / magasins	
▬ ▬ Waterfront Trail - Off-road / Hors route	❓ Information / Renseignements	Conservation Area / Zone de protection de la nature	
🚩 Alerts / Alertes	☀ Lookout / Vue panoramique	Provincial Park / Parc provincial de l'Ontario	
▼2.0▼ Distance / Distance (km)	⚓ Marina / Marina		
▬▬▬ Other Trails - Connection / Liaison	℗ Parking / Stationnement	Built-up / Secteur bâti	
H Hospital / Hôpital	🏛 Town Hall / Hôtel de ville	✝ Cemetery / Cimetière	
● Attraction / Attraction	🚻 Washrooms / W.-C.	Park, Natural Area / Parc, Espace naturel	
⚓ Beach / Plage			

Map 6-6: Grand Bend

Great Lakes
Waterfront Trail

Map 6-6 Carte

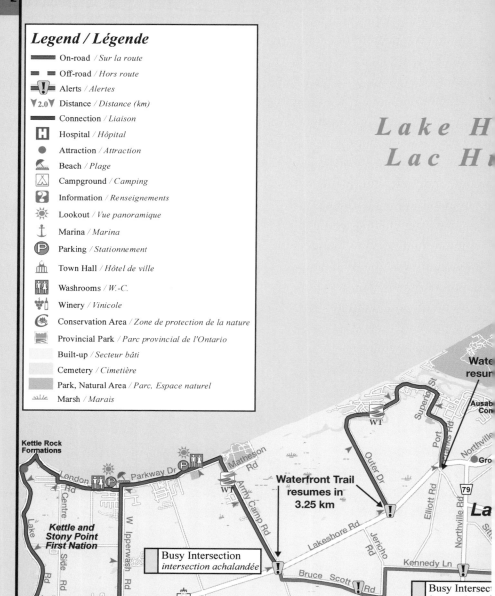

Legend / Légende

- ━━━ On-road / *Sur la route*
- ▬ ▬ Off-road / *Hors route*
- Alerts / *Alertes*
- ▼2.0▼ Distance / *Distance (km)*
- ━━━ Connection / *Liaison*
- H Hospital / *Hôpital*
- ● Attraction / *Attraction*
- Beach / *Plage*
- Campground / *Camping*
- Information / *Renseignements*
- Lookout / *Vue panoramique*
- Marina / *Marina*
- P Parking / *Stationnement*
- Town Hall / *Hôtel de ville*
- Washrooms / *W.-C.*
- Winery / *Vinicole*
- Conservation Area / *Zone de protection de la nature*
- Provincial Park / *Parc provincial de l'Ontario*
- Built-up / *Secteur bâti*
- Cemetery / *Cimetière*
- Park, Natural Area / *Parc, Espace naturel*
- Marsh / *Marais*

Lake H
Lac Hu

Wate
resur

Ausab
Con

WT

Kettle Rock
Formations

London
Parkway Dr

Matheson
Rd

Superior St

Port
Frances Rd

Outer Dr

Northville

Gro

Waterfront Trail
resumes in
3.25 km

Elliott Rd

Northville Rd

79

La

Kettle and
Stony Point
First Nation

W Ippperwash Rd

Army Camp Rd

WT

Lakeshore Rd

Jericho
Rd

Kennedy Ln

Busy Intersection
intersection achalandée

Bruce Scott Rd

Busy Intersec
intersection ac

Indian Ln

21

Map 6-6: Grand Bend

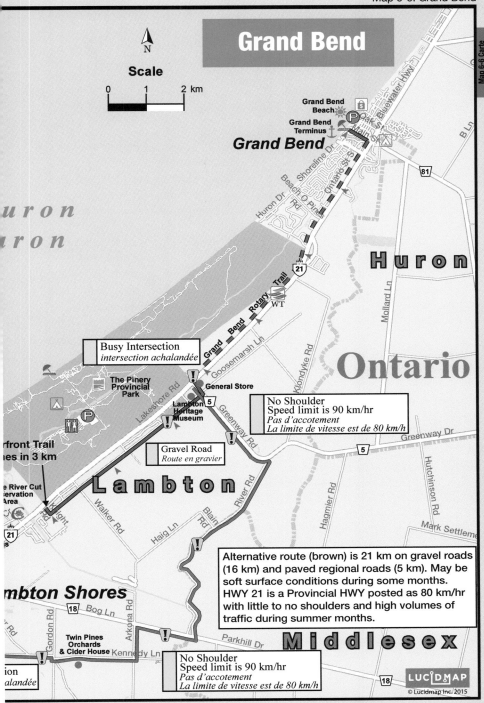

Grand Bend

Scale

0   1   2 km

Grand Bend Beach
Grand Bend Terminus
Grand Bend

Old Bluewater Hwy

Map 6-6 Carte

H u r o n

81

Busy Intersection
intersection achalandée

The Pinery Provincial Park

General Store

No Shoulder
Speed limit is 90 km/hr
Pas d'accotement
La limite de vitesse est de 80 km/h

Lambton Heritage Museum

Gravel Road
Route en gravier

front Trail
es in 3 km

e River Cut
ervation
Area

O n t a r i o

Greenway Dr

L a m b t o n

21

Alternative route (brown) is 21 km on gravel roads
(16 km) and paved regional roads (5 km). May be
soft surface conditions during some months.
HWY 21 is a Provincial HWY posted as 80 km/hr
with little to no shoulders and high volumes of
traffic during summer months.

mbton Shores

18   Bog Ln

Twin Pines
Orchards
& Cider House   Kennedy Ln

Parkhill Dr   **M i d d l e s e x**

No Shoulder
Speed limit is 90 km/hr
Pas d'accotement
La limite de vitesse est de 80 km/h

18

ion
alandée

LUC[D]MAP
© Lucidmap Inc. 2015

89

Plan Your Adventure

Plan your Trip on the Great Lakes Waterfront Trail

Whether you have two weeks, two days or two hours, you can find excellent trip plans on the following websites:

Great Lakes Waterfront Trail . . . . www.waterfronttrail.org
Ontario's Southwest . . . . www.ontariossouthwest.com
CAA Southwest . . . . www.caasco.com/Auto/Road-Trip
Ontario by Bike . . . . www.ontariobybike.ca
Tourism Sarnia Lambton . . . . www.tourismsarnialambton.com
Tourism Windsor Essex Pelee Island . . . . visitwindsoressex.com
Chatham-Kent Tourism . . . . www.chatham-kent.ca/tourism
Tourism Elgin County . . . . www.elgintourist.com
Norfolk County Tourism . . . . www.norfolktourism.ca
Tourism Haldimand . . . . tourism.haldimandcounty.on.ca
Niagara Parks . . . . www.niagaraparks.com
Niagara Cycling Tourism Centre . . . . www.niagaracyclingtourism.com

Camping in Provincial Parks and Conservation Areas

Listed in geographical order from Grand Bend to Niagara.

The Pinery Provincial Park, Grand Bend, Lambton Shores
Mooretown Campground, Mooretown, St. Clair Township
Cathcart Park and Campground, Sombra, St. Clair Township
Branton Cundick Park and Campground, Sombra, St. Clair Township
Holiday Beach Conservation Area, Amherstburg
East Park Campground, Pelee Island
Wheatley Provincial Park, Chatham-Kent
Rondeau Provincial Park, Chatham-Kent
Port Burwell Provincial Park, Port Burwell, Bayhem, Elgin
Long Point Provincial Park, Port Rowan, Norfolk
Backus Heritage Conservation Area, Port Rowan, Norfolk
Turkey Point, Provincial Park, Norfolk
Norfolk Conservation Area, Norfolk
Haldimand Conservation Area, Selkirk, Haldimand
Selkirk Provincial Park, Selkirk, Haldimand
Byng Island Conservation Area, Dunnville, Haldimand
Rock Point Provincial Park, Haldimand
Long Beach Conservation Area, Wainfleet, Niagara

The Waterfront Regeneration Trust (WRT) leads a partnership of 100+ communities committed to the creation of the Great Lakes Waterfront Trail. In addition, the WRT is grateful to have partners and volunteers who contribute not only funding but also time, knowledge and ideas in our efforts to complete, expand and promote the Great Lakes Waterfront Trail.

Conservation Authorities

- *St. Clair Region Conservation Authority*
- *Essex Region Conservation Authority*
- *Kettle Creek Conservation Authority*
- *Lower Thames Valley Conservation Authority*
- *Upper Thames River Conservation Authority*
- *Long Point Conservation Authority*
- *Grand River Conservation Authority*
- *Niagara Peninsula Conservation Authority*

Founding Funding Partners for the Lake Erie and Lake Huron Waterfront Trail:

- *CAA*
- *Ontario's Southwest*
- *Ontario Trillium Foundation*
- *Province of Ontario*
- *League of Waterfront Trail Champions:*
  Marty Bernstein
  Diane Brodeur
  Dennis Findlay
  Marilyn Mann
  Elaine Theriault
  David Werezak

Trail Organizations:

- *Bluewater Trails*
- *St. Clair River Trail*
- *Lambton Shores Nature Trail*

NGOs:

- *Ontario By Bike*
- *Venture Niagara*
- *Share the Road Coalition Canada*

Waterfront Regeneration Trust

Protecting, Enhancing, and Celebrating the Great Lakes

Founded by the Honourable David Crombie and established in 1988 the Waterfront Regeneration Trust (WRT) is the charitable organization leading the movement for waterfront regeneration by creating a Great Lakes Waterfront Trail. We do this in partnership with close to 100 community partners, conservation authorities, the Province of Ontario, many community groups and donors.

The Great Lakes are the largest group of freshwater lakes on earth, containing 21% of the world's surface freshwater. In Canada, they are unique to Ontario and one of our most precious resources. The WRT is committed to connecting people to their Great Lakes waterfront and in doing so, engaging them in the work of making our Great Lakes waterfront a healthy and vibrant place to live, work and visit.

To support this work, please visit www.WaterfrontTrail.org and donate.